THE EVERYDAY WHEAT-FREE & GLUTEN-FREE COOKBOOK

THE EVERYDAY WHEAT-FREE & GLUTEN-FREE COOKBOOK

Michelle Berriedale-Johnson

KEY PORTER BOOKS

This edition published in 2000 by Key Porter Books Limited.
First published in 1998 in the United Kingdom by Grub Street, London, England.

Canadian Cataloguing in Publication Data

Berriedale-Johnson, Michelle
    The everyday wheat-free & gluten-free cookbook : recipes for celiacs & wheat intolerants

ISBN 1-55263-131-1

1. Wheat-free diet - Recipes. 2. Gluten-free diet - Recipes. I. Title.

RM237.86.B47 2000   641.5′631   C99-933026-8

Key Porter Books Limited
70 The Esplanade
Toronto, ON M5E 1R2

www.keyporter.com

Photography: Simon Smith
Design and formatting: Adam Denchfield Design

The publisher would like to thank the Canadian Celiac Association for all their help and advice in the preparation of this book.

00 01 02 03 6 5 4 3 2 1

Contents

Introduction

Even if you only read the occasional women's magazine, you cannot have failed to notice that it has at least one article in every issue on food-related health. It could be an allergy, or candida; it could be food related to depression, or to asthma, or to arthritis, or to your child's failure to do well at school - or to almost anything else!

But why this obsession with food? Well, the proposition that "we are what we eat" seems a fairly reasonable one to most people. But what are we eating? Food scandals over the last few years have become more and more frequent. The salmonella and eggs scandal; BSE or mad cow disease; listeria in soft cheese; E. coli poisoning from cooked meats. And what about the genetic modification of our food? Or the pesticide residues which were recently so high that we were advised to peel our carrots so as to avoid eating the pesticides left on the surface? Or the antibiotics fed so regularly to animals that they are no longer effective when used to treat humans?

Those are only the food scandals which hit the headlines. Sophisticated, highly technical food manufacturing and plant-breeding techniques over the last fifty years have changed our food almost beyond recognition. More importantly, they have meant that nearly all the food we eat has been processed may times, subject to violent changes in heat, while its ingredients have had their chemical structures altered to achieve what are thought to be better textures or better tastes.

As yet we really do not know exactly what effects these changes have had on our bodies. But we do know that they have come extremely quickly (in fifty years) and that animals (including humans) evolve very slowly - over thousands of years. So there is a good chance that our bodies have a problem coping with such dramatic changes.

As far as the subject of this book is concerned - wheat and gluten allergy or intolerance - this rapid change is very relevant.

Gluten, found primarily in wheat, oats, rye, barley and triticum, is a gluey substance which is enormously useful to food manufacturers as it does, literally, glue or bind ingredients together. Gluten holds together the flour which makes bread, for example, when the yeast expands to make the bread dough rise. Gluten stops sauces or soups curdling while it gives a smooth texture to cheese spread and dips, dressings, margarines, sweets, tinned meats, mustard and a thousand other products on the supermarket shelves.

It has therefore been in the manufacturers' interests to use it extensively - and in growers' interest to increase the gluten content of grains, especially those grown in Canada and the UK.

Some medical practitioners see gluten as one of the main trouble makers in the modern diet. Because it is a type of protein, the body tries to absorb it in the same way that it absorbs other nutrition-bearing proteins. But, unfortunately, because of its natural stickiness, it can clog up our guts and get, undigested, into our bloodstreams.

For individuals with celiac disease, gluten presents a particular problem as it damages the internal lining of their digestive tracts. For those with an allergy to wheat, the situation is slightly different as there is no certainty as to which constituent of the wheat is upsetting them - or maybe it is no particular constituent but the combination of individual elements which make up the wheat grain.

The conditions of celiac disease and wheat allergy are often confused as the symptoms and treatment for both conditions are very similar. As an added complication, the symptoms for both vary enormously and the longer patients remain undiagnosed, the sicker they are likely to become and the more varied their symptoms are likely to be!

The most obvious of these symptoms are usually digestive and run as follows:

- Diarrhoea (and occasionally constipation)
- Bloating
- Abdominal pain
- Flatulence
- Nausea and vomiting

However, there is another batch of common symptoms of both conditions which do not relate to the digestion:

- Chronic fatigue
- Weight loss
- Lactose intolerance
- Bone pain
- Depression

Psychological problems are not uncommon. And, as if that were not enough:

- Headaches
- Mouth ulcers
- Asthma
- Fainting and chest pains
- have all also been caused by a gluten intolerance.

In babies and small children there are other indications, especially of celiac disease. These are:

- General failure to thrive
- Diarrhoea
- Bloating
- Vomiting
- Fatty and smelly stools

There is also an increasing amount of evidence to suggest that gluten intolerance could be very important in childhood psychological disorders such as hyperactivity and autism.

CELIAC DISEASE

Celiac disease is not, medically speaking, an intolerance or allergy but an auto-immune disease. It can occur in babies, children or adults and is a state in which a person's immune system reacts against a substance that they touch, breathe or, in the case of celiac disease, eat.

In the case of someone with celiac disease, the immune system reacts against the protein called gluten found in wheat, rye, barley and possibly oats. The gluten damages the lining of the small intestine.

A normal small intestine is covered with tiny fingerlike fronds or protrusions called villi, which absorb nutrients from food. In celiac disease, one element of the protein gluten (called gliadin) damages the villi so badly that they are flattened into little humps and are unable to absorb nutrients at all. This is why untreated celiacs, apart from their other symptoms, will continue to lose weight. In most cases, as soon as gluten is removed from the diet the villi recover and continue to behave as normal. If the condition remains untreated for a long time, however, the villi may be so badly damaged that they will never entirely recover their full function.

HISTORY

The Roman physician Galen described a condition in which the digestion was upset by farinaceous foods (foods containing gluten) as early as the second century BC. In the 19th century carbohydrates (including gluten-bearing farinaceous food) in general were thought to be the problem. In fact, it is possible that total carbohydrate intolerance may still be a problem for the relatively small number of people who do not get well when they stop eating gluten.

Nineteenth-century patients were put on a no-carbohydrate, high-fat diet - a terribly difficult diet to follow! Matters improved when, in the 1920s, two American doctors discovered that their patients could eat bananas and banana flour (even though bananas are very high in carbohydrates) without being ill.

However, it was the terrible food shortages suffered by the Dutch during the Second World War that pointed the finger at gluten rather than total carbohydrates. For a long period during the war there was no regular gluten bread to be had in Holland - and celiacs all over the country got better!

By the 1950s new biopsy techniques allowed doctors to remove a sample from the small intestine so that they could examine the gluten-flattened villi in detail. This made diagnosis relatively straightforward.

TREATMENT

Once you have been diagnosed as a celiac, the treatment is simple - stay off gluten. This may sound easy but it is not, mainly because of the very widespread use of gluten in food processing I talked about earlier. However, it is very important that if you are a celiac, you do keep rigidly to your gluten-free diet as your body, especially if you have suffered from the condition for a long time before diagnosis, will be extremely sensitive and will react to the tiniest amount of gluten with a dramatic return of your symptoms.

If, as a diagnosed celiac, you do not improve on a gluten-free diet, it is worth looking into other food sensitivities (dairy, soya, fish or almost any food you eat regularly). If your gut lining (the skin on the inside of your intestine) was badly damaged before you were diagnosed, it may still be "leaky," allowing other food molecules to which you may be sensitive into your bloodstream. If your body is low in zinc, this can make the problem worse.

THE OAT QUESTION

Gluten is found in most grains (wheat, barley, rye and oats - though not rice) so grain is effectively off the menu for celiacs. There is, however, a query over oats. Although oats are a grain, they do not contain gliadin but a gliadin analogue (an identikit gliadin) called avelin and it is not certain whether this actually affects celiacs. Medical trials carried out in Finland suggest that it does not, but these trials are not comprehensive. Nor are doctors sure whether, although celiacs may show no immediate reaction to avelin, it might do them some long-term damage. Medical advice therefore is to be extremely careful: if you are badly affected by celiac disease, are elderly or are a child, it is probably wiser to take no risks and stay off oats as well as the other grains. However, no recipes including oats appear in this book.

DERMATITIS HERPETIFORMIS

There is a fairly rare form of dermatitis called Dermatitis Herpetiformis, whose symptoms are itchy patches on the elbows and back of the knees, followed by the lower back and other parts of the body. This is also caused by damaged villi and its treatment is exactly the same as for celiac disease - no gluten.

WHEAT INTOLERANCE

Wheat intolerance falls into a quite separate medical "compartment" from celiac disease as it is a food intolerance rather than an auto-immune condition. Essentially, this means that you should be able to recover from it although there are a few people who are so badly affected they will need to remain wheat-free for good.

WHY DO FOOD INTOLERANCES OCCUR?

There are no definite answers as to why people develop food intolerances although it seems clear that over-indulgence combined with a depressed immune system is usually at least part of the cause. Nationally people tend to be most intolerant to the foods they eat most. In northern Europe the main intolerances are to dairy products and wheat; in North America to corn; in the Far East to soya and so on.

It also seems pretty clear that a healthy person can eat most foods without a problem but if they stop being healthy - if they suffer a gastro-intestinal or viral illness, are involved in an accident of some kind, suffer a bereavement or family break-up, are overworked, over-tired, or over-stressed, are not properly nourished (in terms of vitamins and minerals - not calories!) and so on - their bodies become less able to cope. At that point they may react badly to foods which under normal circumstances they could eat with no problems.

In medical terms, this could be because they are no longer producing the correct amount or type of the enzymes needed to break down and digest the food. Food may not therefore be properly "processed" before it enters the bloodstream. It is also possible that as a result of their illness, the lining of their guts or intestines may have become "leaky," thus allowing undigested proteins into the bloodstream and thereby setting up intolerant reactions.

With regard to wheat in particular, there are two theories why we should react to an excess. One is that humans are omnivores, designed to eat a wide variety of foods but that the diet of the late 20th century has come to rely far too greatly on wheat and the by-products of wheat.

The other is the "hunter-gatherer" theory, which says that our bodies are basically designed to eat meat (hunted) and wild fruits and nuts (gathered). Although we became domesticated some 10,000 years ago when we settled down and started to cultivate grains, in evolutionary terms this is no time at all, and our systems have just not yet got used to this new grain-based diet.

PREVALENCE OF WHEAT AND WHEAT BY-PRODUCTS IN OUR DIETS

Whichever - if either - is right, there is no doubt that wheat and wheat by-products (wheat starch and gluten) have all but taken over our diets. Popular "western" type food, which is rapidly displacing many traditional third world diets, depends largely on wheaten bread, wheat-based pastas and pizzas, wheat-based biscuits and cakes - and those are only the products where the wheat content is obvious.

As I said earlier, the gluey, elastic substance or gluten which is left after the starch in wheat flour is washed away is enormously useful in the general processing and manufacture of food.

TREATMENT

Someone who is wheat intolerant may be reacting to the gluten in wheat or to some other protein but as with celiac disease, the primary treatment for wheat intolerance is to stop eating wheat! If your digestion (or indeed any part of your body) is under stress, constantly making it do things - or eat things - which it finds difficult, is only going to put it under yet more stress.

Stopping doing those stressful things - or eating those stress-creating foods - even if only for a short while, will give the body a break and a chance to rebuild its own strength. You can help it with plenty of rest, lots of good nutritious food that it can tolerate and reducing any other stresses that may be under your control. Once your general health has improved, you can start gradually re-introducing the problem foods and there is a good chance that they will be perfectly well tolerated. However, even if you make a total recovery it would be wise to limit your intake of wheat - or whatever food proved to cause sensitivity - in the future so as to avoid getting into an "overload" situation again.

DIAGNOSIS

If you suspect that you are suffering from a wheat or gluten intolerance, your first port of call should be your general practitioner. Because celiac disease is well recognized if your symptoms fall within the list on page 2, your GP may automatically refer you to a gastro-enterologist who will perform the normal tests for celiac disease (physical examination, medical history, blood samples, etc.) ending up with a biopsy. However, you would do well to read up on the subject yourself as well so that you are able to ask the right questions of both your GP and specialist.

But although you may be reacting to wheat, you may not be a celiac - which is good news for you as it means both that your diet will not be quite so restricted, and that you probably will get better. However, because food intolerance in general is a relatively uncharted territory as far as most GPs are concerned, you may have more difficulty convincing him or her that wheat could be your problem. If so, you might want to visit either your local community dietitian (check with your GP practice or your local hospital) or a qualified nutritionist (see page 201 for referral agencies).

Whatever you do, do **not** set off on any kind of exclusion diet without qualified medical advice. This is especially important if you are dealing with a child, an elderly person or anyone who is already on medication or suffers from some other health problem. *It is particularly important when dealing with a possible food intolerance that one maintains a balanced and varied diet* - and to achieve this when you are cutting out a large swathe of what you normally eat will require experienced professional advice.

REVIEWING YOUR LIFESTYLE

What you can do for yourself is to review your lifestyle. There are, no doubt, a few people who have got themselves totally sorted out. They make time for exercise and relaxation, minimize their stress levels through meditation or long walks with the dog, eat a good balanced diet at the right time - and do not overdose on caffeine or cheap red wine! But most of us fall down in some area. And if we get ill and overstressed, far from taking more care of ourselves, all too often we drive ourselves even harder to compensate for our perceived inefficiencies - thus making the whole situation worse.

It is not unheard of for allergy and intolerance problems to disappear all by themselves when the person concerned makes serious changes to their lifestyle and allows themselves a bit of that "tender loving care" so many of them shower on others.

TAKING ON YOUR OWN CATERING

The other thing that wheat intolerants and celiacs will undoubtedly have to do, once they have sorted out a sensible diet to pursue, is to take responsibility for their own food. This may sound an odd thing to say, but the arrival of convenience food on the shelves has meant that we really do not need to think about what we eat at all. If the picture on the pack looks good, we take it home, pop it in the microwave - and eat. But that is no good if you are on what effectively is an exclusion diet.

READING THE LABELS

For a start you will need to learn to recognize your gastronomic *bête noir* - and this may not be that easy. Gluten, wheat starch and their derivatives are extremely widely used in the food industry but they are rarely labelled as "Wheat - beware." However, supermarkets are becoming increasingly aware of food intolerance problems and several now highlight potentially allergenic ingredients on their own label packs.

Breads, cakes and biscuits are obviously a no-go area - but be careful of breads apparently made of other ingredients such as rye (fine for wheat intolerants, no good for celiacs) as they may well have wheat flour in there as well. Always read the label with care before buying.

However, your reading cannot stop there as the most unlikely foods may contain a wheat by-product. Moreover, you need to know what you are looking for, as it is not always obvious. Below is a list of wheat and gluten derivatives, plus unexpected foods where you may, though not always, find them.

You must always check the ingredients list.

- Barley
- Bran
- Cereal filler
- Commercial salad dressings
- Couscous
- Curry powder
- Farina
- Fruit drinks
- Horseradish creams/sauces
- HPP
- Instant hot drinks - coffee, tea, chocolate
- Ketchups
- Luncheon or other prepared meats
- Malt
- Modified starch
- Mustards - English and some French
- Oats
- Rye
- Sausages
- Sauces - most commercially made sauces or sauce mixes
- Seasoning mixes
- Semolina
- Soups - most commercially made tinned, chilled or frozen soups
- Soy sauce and most other Chinese sauces, except those marked wheat free/gluten free
- Starch
- Sweets - any sweets which contain grains and any which contain stabilizers made from gluten
- Wheat flour
- Pepper in restaurants

Then you have the problem of foods which are not labelled at all - the succulent-looking sausages in the butcher's, or the coated cod fillets in the fish market. The sausages may contain fillers, the fish coated in batter or breadcrumbs - both off the menu. So if there is no label you must ask - and not be satisfied with a vague answer. For example, you must make sure that the butcher claiming to make gluten-free sausages really does understand about possible contamination with other wheat or gluten products.

If your exclusion diet is to work and you are to get better, you must be rigorous.

THE REVIVAL OF HOME COOKERY

The result of all this is that you will inevitably have to make by far the greater part of your food yourself at home. Gone are the days of convenience foods. The up-side to this is that you will probably be eating much healthier and tastier food - and that you may really get a buzz out of cooking!

This may sound fine to someone who is a good and interested cook - but like a nightmare to someone who has difficulty in heating the baked beans without burning them. But things will improve.

Cooking is not some magic art but a very practical and logical skill, quite easily acquired - especially if you have a vested interest in the end result tasting good!

Some foods are very easy to adapt to a gluten- or wheat-free diet - potato flour, for example, is just as good a thickener for any kind of sauce or custard (some people would say better) as wheat flour. Other areas are really quite difficult. It is just not possible to produce the equivalent of an ordinary commercial white loaf of bread, without gluten. One can bake bread, and very nice bread too (you will find a series of recipes in the recipe section and suppliers of ready baked bread in the resources section) but it will be different bread.

Not that this is necessarily a bad thing. There is a strong chance that the reason you ended up with a wheat intolerance or even celiac disease is because you ate a good deal too much wheat and wheat by-products in the first place. So a good way to ensure that you do not do so again is to broaden your tastes.

BUYING GOOD INGREDIENTS

The ingredients that you can use are obviously going to be limited by your diet - and some may have to come from specialist or mail order suppliers. (See Resource list on page 202) However, in general, try to buy as good quality food as you can.

There is a strong argument being made by both medical practitioners and environmentalists that one of the reasons we are seeing such a rise in food allergies and degenerative diseases is the enormous cocktail of chemicals (pesticides, fertilizers, post-harvest treatments, etc.) with which we drench the food we eat.

The one way you can avoid this situation is by buying and cooking your own "organically" grown food (free of all chemical fertilizers, pesticides, herbicides and post-harvest treatments, or hormones and antibiotics in meat). Organic food is now a lot easier to find than it once was, and although it is still more expensive than conventionally grown or raised products it may be worth the money if it really helps you get better.

EATING OUT

One of the hardest things for those on exclusion diets to come to terms with is eating out - either in restaurants or with friends. Either they become paranoid (with reason, often) that what they are eating may contain something that they should not have, or they become so embarrassed by the situation that they will not go out at all. But this is a great shame - and quite unnecessary.

There was a time, not too long ago, when asking a restaurant to leave something out of a dish was just regarded as weird, but things are a lot better now. Food allergy has had so much publicity over the last few years that most restaurants are aware that it does exist and do at least try to be helpful.

If you are planning a meal out, call the restaurant in advance, explain your situation and ask what they have on their menu which might be suitable for you, or which they could adapt for you. Do make clear to them that this is a serious illness and that it would be dangerous for you to eat any of your forbidden foods. However, you must be aware of the hidden ingredients and point them out - you cannot expect either a chef or restaurant manager to be an expert in gluten intolerance! If the restaurant is not prepared to be helpful - go elsewhere. Or, if you have no option, take your own food and tell them what you will be doing and why.

If you decide to eat out and do not have a chance to call ahead, examine everything on the menu very carefully. Go for things which are unlikely to contain wheat - no sauces or thickened soups, for example - but still ask for the exact ingredients. Explain once again that you have an illness and that it is really important that you eat the right food. There is no legal requirement for a restaurant to provide accurate details of ingredients to their customers, but hopefully that will soon change.

If you are travelling, so likely to have to eat out a lot, carry your own emergency rations with you - packets of gluten-free cookies and muffins are always a great standby. Obviously, the longer you are travelling, the more you will need to take but you will soon discover what you need to survive - and what you are likely to be unable to get on the road!

If eating with friends, be sure to give them plenty of warning of what you can and cannot have. Your friends may be quite happy to cook something that you, along with everyone else, can eat, but if they sound at all dubious, suggest that you take along your own food. That way you will feel relaxed because you know you will not be eating anything that you shouldn't - and your host will feel equally relaxed because he or she will know they are not feeding you anything which will make you ill.

BABIES, CHILDREN AND TEENAGERS

Having a celiac baby can be quite unnerving as you may well be a new and inexperienced parent. However, if your baby shows any of the classic symptoms (failure to thrive and gain weight, smelly stools, diarrhoea, vomiting or bloating, general "unwellness") go immediately to your GP. As soon as your baby is diagnosed and gluten removed from his or her diet, matters should start to improve immediately. Do not, however, be tempted to overfeed to make up for lost time. Babies can catch up in lost growth very easily.

If your child is celiac, or has a wheat allergy and it persists, you will then find yourself with a toddler on a special diet. You obviously want to ensure that your child will not eat foods which will make him or her ill, but neither do you want to turn them into an "oddity." This should be reasonably easy at home as you should be able to convert the whole family to a mainly gluten-free diet - although this may be a little more difficult if there are older children who are free of dietary problems. However, as far as possible, make sure that all the foods you have at home are wheat- and gluten-free - and if your child brings home friends from school, serve the friends with the same food you are all eating. They may not even notice the difference.

However, with small children you must make sure that all their relatives, their friends' parents and their school are aware of their condition. Your child must also be aware of the fact that when away from home, he or she must be careful and that eating things on the forbidden list will just make them feel horrible.

Make sure that they never go out without a stock of their favourite wheat- or gluten-free snacks, biscuits or drinks so that when others are eating, they can too. You will also need to arrange with the school either for them to have a gluten- or wheat-free meal or, if that is going to be difficult, for them to take a pack lunch with them.

As your toddler grows into his or her teens, you may find that they are tempted to lapse from their diets. This could be because the teen years are a time when many kids wish to establish their independence - and refusing to stick to the diet their parents have suggested may be one way. Other teenagers are acutely embarrassed by being seen to be "different" from their friends. Some may become lazy and not wish to bother with cooking or finding special food. Others may not react too badly to a bit of gluten or wheat in their diet and therefore assume that they need no longer bother with their diet.

Celiac disease does not go away so your teenager will always remain sensitive to gluten.

PREGNANCY AND CHILDBEARING

Whatever they may do in their teenage years, however, both boys and girls wishing to have a family will need to watch their diet. Untreated celiac disease can cause infertility in men. As far as women are concerned, it may make it more difficult for them to become pregnant, easier for them to miscarry and may cause an acute form of anaemia during their pregnancy.

A FEW WARNING WORDS

- Always eat before you go out to a party so if there is nothing there that you can eat you will not be racked with pangs of hunger all night. Or better yet, check with your host ahead of time.
- Always carry a snack with you when you go out - in case your plans change and you cannot find anything that you are allowed to eat. You can always drink water if there is nothing else but if there are only sandwiches to eat you are stuck!
- Never accept someone's word that the food they are offering you is wheat- or gluten-free unless you are really sure they know what they are saying - people often assure you things are safe when they really do not know.
- If you have to go into hospital, check with the hospital what their provision of wheat- or gluten-free food may be - there is no guarantee they will be able to provide it. You may either need to get a family member or friend to cook your own food and bring it in - or prepare lots for yourself before-hand and bring it in with you.
- Do not be tempted, just because you are feeling so much better, to assume that you are cured! There is no cure for celiac disease, and even wheat intolerants may have to spend a couple of years avoiding wheat before their system will tolerate it again. Be warned that if your body has just started to recover it will be even more sensitive to the food it didn't like, and its reaction will be dramatic.

THE RECIPES

The recipes which follow are, naturally, all wheat- and gluten-free. However, they are not all for dishes that you would normally expect to contain either wheat or gluten. Since it is recognized that over-indulgence is one of the causes of food intolerance, one of the first things that the wheat intolerant or celiac should do is try to broaden their diet. And it is amazing, once you start to look around, how many dishes there are which do not contain and never have contained either wheat or gluten.

There are, of course, many recipes for foods which you would naturally expect to be made of wheat flour: cakes, biscuits, pastries, pastas, sauces, thickened soups, etc. Although there are a number of wheat- and/or gluten-free "mixes" on the market, we have chosen (with the exception of pasta) to use "natural" ingredients rather than packet mixes. This is partially because we feel that if you are to start a new regime cooking yourself real food, you should cook with real food, and partly because the mixes tend to be a great deal more expensive than the raw materials.

With regard to pasta, you can make your own and indeed may need to do so if you live away from a main centre - it will also be a lot cheaper than buying it ready made. However, it is a good deal more bother so we normally suggest using one of the quite wide range of commercial brands available either in health food stores or via mail order - see page 202.

My "raw materials" have been gram or chick pea flour (used widely in Indian cooking), rice flour, maize flour or cornmeal, potato flour and cornflour, soya flour and buckwheat flour. However, you should check with your suppliers that the latter are not milled with wheat flour and if they are, the risk of contamination may be quite great.

Of all the baked goods, cakes, when excluding wheat flour, work the best and I would defy anyone to tell that many of the cakes in the cake section were not made with wheat flour.

Pastry and biscuits work pretty well although the lack of gluten prevents them holding together as well as a wheat-based mixture. However, as long as you are prepared to put up with them being a bit crumbly, the flavour is very good.

Potato flour or cornstarch makes very successful thickeners for sauces, soups or anything else.

The only area which presents real problems is bread, especially as we have got used to the very risen, soft breads which depend heavily on a high gluten content. There are recipes for half a dozen delicious and well-textured breads in the baking section of the book (thanks to the ingenuity and skills of my good friend and colleague Miriam Polunin) - but they are not, and never will be, Wonderbread!

Dishes which do not, and never did, use wheat flour speak for themselves.

A final note: You will see the abbreviation hpd, used in some of the recipes: this means heaped. All other spoonfuls are level. The imperial measurements are British and in most respects are the same as in North America. However, note that the British pint is 20 ounces, the British quart is about 40 ounces.

Happy Cooking!

Soups, Starters and Light Lunches

*Sweet Potato Soup with
Coriander and Ginger*

Cream of Mushroom Soup

*Creamed Green Pea Soup
with Pine Nuts*

Kidney Soup

Leek, Potato and Smoked Mackerel Soup

Bacon, Apple and Sausage Pie

Smoked Fish Pâté

Seedy Pastry Squares

Red Pepper Pâté

Terrine of Chicken and Walnuts

Polenta with Gorgonzola

Steamed Potatoes with Walnut Sauce

Salmon Mousse with Green Peppercorns

Eggs Florentine

Cheese Sables

Herb and Bacon Casserole

Crudités and Dips

French Toast

Vol Au Vent Cases

Not only are sweet potatoes delicious to eat but they are an excellent source of Vitamin E, potassium and iron. The orange variety are also high in the anti-oxidant vitamins and are thought to be protective against cancer.

Sweet Potato Soup with Coriander and Ginger

Serves 6

This is the most wonderfully coloured soup for a cold evening - yet works equally well chilled on a hot summer night!

600 g	sweet potato	1 lb 5oz
200 g	ordinary potatoes	7oz
2 cm	cube fresh ginger root, peeled	1 inch
4	large cloves of garlic	4
1 L	water	1¾ pints
100 mL	medium sherry	3½ fl oz
	salt	
	pepper	
	large bunch of fresh coriander	

Peel the sweet potato and scrub the ordinary potatoes. Cut them into large dice and put them in a deep pot with the fresh ginger root, the garlic cloves, peeled but whole, and the water. Bring to the boil and simmer for 30 - 40 minutes or until the vegetables are thoroughly cooked. Purée in a food processor then return to the pan, add the sherry and season to taste with salt and pepper. Just before serving add the chopped coriander.

PER SERVING	
Energy Kcals	137.33
Protein g	2.32
Fat g	.42
Saturated fatty acids g	.45
Monounsaturated fatty acids g	1.38
Polyunsaturated fatty acids g	.15
Carbohydrate g	28.61
Total Sugars g	6.67
Sodium mg	173.49
Fibre g	3.00

If you want a puréed rather than a "bitty" soup, put the mixture through a blender or food processor, then sieve it before returning it to the pan, adding the cream and adjusting the seasoning.

Cream of Mushroom Soup

Serves 6

A classic mushroom soup which is given a lovely fresh flavour by the lemon juice.

1/2	a Spanish onion, very thinly sliced	1/2
30 mL	olive oil	2 tbsp
225 g	button mushrooms, thinly sliced	8 oz
	juice 1 lemon	
15 mL	corn starch	1 tbsp
600 mL	chicken stock	1 pint
300 mL	milk	1/2 pint
150 mL	dry white wine	5 fl oz
100 mL	whipping cream	4 fl oz
	salt	
	pepper	

Heat the oil in a heavy pan and gently cook the onion until it is transparent and softening but not coloured. When the onion is soft, add the mushrooms and lemon juice and cook them altogether for a couple of minutes; do not let them brown. Add the corn starch, stir around for a minute or two, then gradually add the stock, milk and white wine. Bring the mixture to the boil and simmer gently for 15 minutes. Season to taste with salt and freshly ground pepper (white if possible). Just before serving add the cream and adjust the seasoning.

PER SERVING	
Energy Kcals	423.91
Protein g	18.11
Fat g	30.61
Saturated fatty acids g	7.01
Monounsaturated fatty acids g	6.80
Polyunsaturated fatty acids g	1.02
Carbohydrate g	16.33
Total Sugars g	5.28
Sodium mg	16468
Fibre g	.44

Although fresh young green peas in summer are a real treat, frozen peas are picked and frozen straight from the plant so are often even fresher than those you shell yourself. The frozen variety also retain all the high levels of vitamins and minerals to be found in the fresh.

Creamed Green Pea Soup with Pine Nuts

Serves 4

This recipe is based on a sixteenth-century Italian dish and is both unusual and delicious. It is also very substantial so could be used as a main course for lunch or a light dinner.

500 g	frozen petits pois	18 oz
4	trimmed spring onions, chopped roughly	4
1	tin of corn (400 g), drained	1
600 mL	chicken stock or water	1 pint
45-60 mL	medium sherry (optional)	3-4 tbsp
30 mL	pine nuts	2 tbsp
30 mL	freshly grated Parmesan	2 tbsp
	sea salt	
	freshly ground black pepper	

Put the peas, with the spring onions and corn in a deep pan and add the stock. Bring to the boil and simmer for 20 minutes. Purée in a food processor or blender. If you want a smooth purée you will also need to put the soup through a sieve to remove the remaining husk; if you would rather a "nuttier" soup, do not sieve. Return the soup to the pan, add the sherry and season to taste with sea salt and freshly ground black pepper.

Meanwhile pulverize the pine nuts in a processor but be careful to be brief as you want them to remain fairly coarse. Mix them with the Parmesan.

To serve, reheat the soup, put it into bowls and scatter each liberally with the pine nut and Parmesan mixture.

PER SERVING	
Energy Kcals	683.25
Protein g	41.24
Fat g	40.04
Saturated fatty acids g	3.55
Polyunsaturated fatty acids g	6.35
Monounsaturated fatty acids g	4.11
Carbohydrate g	38.96
Total Sugars g	9.06
Englyst fibre g	7.90
Sodium mg	631.22

Although offal is no longer very popular it is very nutritious. Kidneys especially are rich in protein, niacin, iron, zinc, copper, selenium and the A and B vitamins. If your family does not like the texture of kidney, cook all the kidneys with the garlic and onion and purée them all together. Their texture will not be so noticeable.

Kidney Soup

Serves 6

A good old-fashioned soup for a cold winter's evening. Eat it round the fire watching the TV or a favourite movie!

45 mL	olive oil	3 tbsp
225 g	onions, sliced thinly	8 oz
2	cloves garlic, chopped finely	2
1	small carrot, diced	1
350 g	lambs' kidneys, trimmed and diced	12 oz
100 g	mushrooms, diced	4 oz
30 mL	fresh parsley, chopped	2 tbsp
2	bay leaves	2
150 mL	port (optional)	5 fl oz
1.2 L	water	2 pints
10 mL	anchovy essence (check that it is gluten free)	2 tsp
5 mL	black peppercorns	1 tsp
	salt	
	pepper	

Heat half the oil in a deep, heavy pan and fry the onion, garlic and carrot briskly until they are lightly tanned and just softening. Then add 225 g/8 oz of the kidneys and the mushrooms and continue to cook, rather more gently, for a couple of minutes or until the kidneys have stopped looking pink.

Add the parsley, bay leaves, port, water, anchovy essence and peppercorns, bring to the boil, cover and simmer gently for 45 minutes. Purée the soup in a processor or blender. Meanwhile, lightly fry the remaining kidney pieces in the rest of the oil. Return the soup to the pan, add the kidney and juice, reheat gently and season to taste with salt and a little more pepper if needed.

PER SERVING	
Energy Kcals	185.24
Protein g	11.01
Fat g	9.39
Saturated fatty acids g	2.01
Monounsaturated fatty acids g	6.26
Polyunsaturated fatty acids g	1.22
Carbohydrate g	7.85
Total Sugars g	6.13
Sodium mg	282.3
Fibre g	1.27

If you have smoked mackerel left over, it makes excellent sandwiches in wheat/gluten-free bread. Just add a squeeze of lemon juice.

Leek, Potato and Smoked Mackerel Soup

Serves 4

"There's eating and drinking", as the saying goes, in this soup. Serve as a main meal with a salad or some cheese to follow.

150 g	leeks, washed, trimmed and sliced	5 oz
300 g	potatoes, scrubbed and diced	10 oz
100 g	peppered smoked mackerel fillets, skinned	4 oz
1 L	water	1¾ pints
150 mL	medium sherry (optional)	5 fl oz

Put the leeks, potatoes and 75 g/3 oz of the mackerel into a large saucepan with the water. Bring to boil and simmer gently for 15 - 20 minutes or until the potatoes are quite cooked. Remove from the pan and purée in a food processor. Return to the saucepan and add the rest of the smoked mackerel, broken into small pieces. You should not need any further seasoning of any kind, but taste to make sure. The soup is delicious just as it is, but if you want you can add chopped parsley or a swirl of cream to each portion just before serving.

PER SERVING	
Energy Kcals	197.25
Protein g	6.94
Fat g	8.06
Saturated fatty acids g	2.36
Monounsaturated fatty acids g	4.90
Polyunsaturated fatty acids g	1.76
Carbohydrate g	15.34
Total Sugars g	2.63
Sodium mg	195.75
Fibre g	1.80

The pie is excellent served warm, in little finger slices, for a cocktail or buffet party.

Bacon, Apple and Sausage Pie

Serves 6

This is an excellent pie for children or for a buffet party. It can be made in advance and frozen or just reheated. It also tastes excellent cold.

150 g	sifted gram (chick pea) flour	9 oz
75 g	butter or low-fat spread suitable for baking	3 oz
30 mL	water	2 tbsp
200 g	bacon, roughly chopped	7 oz
1	medium onion, roughly chopped plus 1 small onion sliced in rings	1
100 g	wheat- and gluten-free sausage meat	4 oz
2	eating apples, peeled	2
	salt	
	pepper	
	pinch dried thyme	
25 g	melted butter	1 oz

Heat the oven to 190°C / 375°F.

Rub the butter or low-fat spread into the flour then mix to a soft dough with 30 - 45 mL/ 2 - 3 tbsps of water. Roll out and line a 20 cm/8 inch pie plate with the pastry. Fry the bacon with the chopped onion in a pan for 5 minutes or until the bacon is beginning to soften and colour slightly. Work in the sausage meat and continue to cook for a further 5 minutes. Add one of the apples, chopped small, a little seasoning and thyme. Spoon the mixture into the middle of the pie crust and spread it out evenly. Slice the rest of the apple and lay it over the sausage mixture along with the onion rings. Brush them all with the melted butter. Bake the pie, uncovered, for 40 - 45 minutes. If the apple and onion look like burning, cover them with a piece of foil. Serve warm or cold with a salad.

PER SERVING	
Energy Kcals	433.09
Protein g	12.48
Fat g	34.39
Saturated fatty acids g	16.80
Monounsaturated fatty acids g	12.48
Polyunsaturated fatty acids g	3.21
Carbohydrate g	19.89
Total Sugars g	2.96
Sodium mg	786.30
Englyst fibre g	3.51

Cheap smoked salmon offcuts are also good in scrambled eggs or in an omelette. You can buy several packets and freeze them for future use.

Smoked Fish Pâté

Serves 6

An excellent standby pâté. You can use the cheap offcuts of smoked salmon available from most supermarkets, if you want to be extravagant.

200 g	smoked mackerel fillet or any other smoked fish of your choice	7 oz
100 g	soft butter	4 oz
100 g	ricotta cheese	4 oz
1½	slices wheat- and gluten-free brown bread - see page 202 or use a proprietary brand	1½
	salt	
	freshly ground black pepper	
	juice of 2 - 3 lemons	

Remove the skin and any bones from the fish and flake it into a mixing bowl with the butter and ricotta. Beat well with a wooden spoon or an electric mixer until they are amalgamated. If you want a very smooth purée you could beat them in a food processor.

Crumb the slices of bread and beat into the pâté.

Season to taste with salt, freshly ground pepper and the lemon juice and serve with rice cakes or gluten- and wheat-free toast.

PER SERVING	
Energy Kcals	287.92
Protein g	8.61
Fat g	25.55
Saturated fatty acids g	12.08
Monounsaturated fatty acids g	8.93
Polyunsaturated fatty acids g	2.82
Carbohydrate g	7.03
Total Sugars g	1.95
Sodium mg	480.33
Fibre g	.46

These would be useful biscuits to carry with you as snacks if you were going out and thought that you would not be able to find any wheat/gluten-free snacks.

Seedy Pastry Squares

Serves 10

These are delicious little biscuits which can be used as cocktail snacks with a drink, as a biscuit with soup or even with cheese.

200 g	sifted gram (chick pea) flour or rice flour or a combination of the two	7 oz
100 g	butter	4 oz
	water	
1	egg, beaten	1
15 mL	sesame, sunflower, poppy seeds or aniseeds	1 tbsp
	sea salt	

Rub the butter into the flour then mix to a soft dough with 30 - 45 mL/ 2 - 3 tablespoons of water. Roll out to approximately 5 mm/¼ inch thickness then paint with the beaten egg. Sprinkle with a little salt and the seed of your choice, cut into squares and bake for 10 - 15 minutes on a greased baking tray, taking great care that they do not burn. Serve warm.

PER SERVING	
Energy Kcals	160.07
Protein g	5.20
Fat g	11.35
Saturated fatty acids g	5.89
Monounsaturated fatty acids g	3.02
Polyunsaturated fatty acids g	1.51
Carbohydrate g	10.10
Total Sugars g	.69
Sodium mg	208.25
Fibre g	2.34

Like any other soft pâté, *Ajwar* can also be used as a dip with fresh vegetable crudités or with a salad.

Red Pepper Pâté

Serves 6

Known as *Ajwar* in southeast Europe (the dish comes from the former Yugoslavia), this pâté uses the sweet red peppers so beloved of the Hungarians, to make a spectacularly coloured and very tasty pâté.

2	medium eggplants, thickly sliced	2
45 mL	olive oil	3 tbsp
2	large red peppers, seeded and chopped	2
3	large cloves of garlic	3
	salt	
	pepper	

In a wide pan fry the eggplant slices in the oil until they are nicely browned on each side. Put all the ingredients except the salt and pepper in a food processor and purée. The pâté should not be totally smooth when processed but have the texture of a country terrine. Season to taste and serve chilled with crackers or toast.

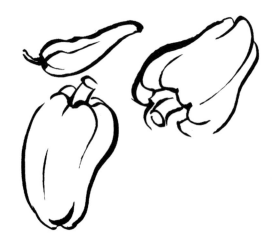

PER SERVING	
Energy Kcals	111.21
Protein g	2.18
Fat g	8.32
Saturated fatty acids g	1.25
Monounsaturated fatty acids g	7.25
Polyunsaturated fatty acids g	1.25
Carbohydrate g	7.61
Total Sugars g	6.77
Sodium mg	70.41
Fibre g	3.84

This terrine is great for a buffet party as it can be eaten with a fork and looks really pretty when laid out on a serving dish with some watercress.

Terrine of Chicken and Walnuts

Serves 6

An old favourite this, as it keeps well and slices excellently for a lunch or buffet party. The walnuts turn a light purple colour as they cook and make the terrine look a lot more interesting!

1	small chicken	1
600 mL	water	1 pint
250 g	bacon	9 oz
50 g	broken walnuts	2 oz
	salt	
10	peppercorns, lightly crushed	10
1	small clove garlic, crushed	1
15 mL	brandy (optional)	1 tbsp

Poach the chicken in the water for 30 - 40 minutes or until it is cooked. Remove the chicken, cool it slightly, then remove the flesh and chop it into reasonably small pieces. Reduce the stock by boiling it fast for about 10 minutes.

Boil the bacon in unsalted water for about 20 minutes or until it is cooked. Cool, then dice it. Mix the chicken in a bowl with the bacon, walnuts, salt, peppercorns, garlic and brandy. Add 75 mL / $\frac{1}{3}$ cup of the reduced stock and mix it well in.

Heat the oven to 180°C/ 350°F .

Grease a round, oval or rectangular terrine dish and spoon the mixture in. Cover and set dish in a pan of water then bake for 75 minutes. Remove the terrine from the oven, cool it slightly then weight it for at least 12 hours.

When it is absolutely cold, turn it out and slice it to serve. Serve as a starter with crackers or gluten-free toast or as a light lunch dish with a salad.

PER SERVING	
Energy Kcals	442.45
Protein g	41.53
Fat g	29.95
Saturated fatty acids g	9.43
Monounsaturated fatty acids g	11.67
Polyunsaturated fatty acids g	7.17
Carbohydrate g	.44
Total Sugars g	.26
Sodium mg	942.76
Fibre g	.33

The polenta is also excellent served warm, buttered and covered with paper-thin slivers of Parmesan.

Polenta with Gorgonzola

Serves 4

Polenta is currently all the rage in smart restaurants - which is great for people who cannot eat wheat or gluten - for once a "special diet" is actually fashionable! Cook the polenta in a non-stick saucepan, if you have one, as otherwise it will glue itself to the pan.

100 g	coarse polenta	4 oz
500 mL	water	18 fl oz
100 g	Gorgonzola	4 oz
	sea salt	

Heat the oven to 180°C / 350°F.

Bring the water to the simmer with the salt. Gradually add the polenta to the water (Italians let it run through their fingers) stirring all the time. Bring back to the simmer and cook, stirring all the time, for 5 minutes. Oil a shallow oven-proof dish and spoon in the polenta mix - the mix should be about 2.5 cm/1 inch deep. Cover with oiled foil and bake for 1 hour.

Take out of the oven and, with the foil still on top, let it get quite cold.

When ready to serve, heat the grill. Turn the polenta out onto a board and slice in thinnish squares - approximately 10 mm/$^{1}/_{2}$ inch thick or cut into triangles. Grill the slices on one side until they are tanned and crisp. Turn the slices and grill lightly on second side. Slice the Gorgonzola and lay it over the polenta. Continue to grill until the cheese is melted and lightly browned.

Serve at once.

PER SERVING	
Energy Kcals	182.00
Protein g	7.25
Fat g	9.18
Saturated fatty acids g	5.18
Monounsaturated fatty acids g	2.00
Polyunsaturated fatty acids g	.38
Carbohydrate g	18.13
Total Sugars g	.25
Sodium mg	612.00
Fibre g	0

Few people think of eating potatoes by themselves although they are really delicious, especially the little early season ones. Try them steamed until just soft and served with melted butter or a good olive oil and freshly grated sea salt.

Steamed Potatoes with Walnut Sauce

Serves 4

This dish hails from South America where the potato is valued as a food in its own right - not just as an accompaniment to other things. Serve it as a light lunch or supper dish as it is rather too substantial for a starter - unless you have a very hungry family!

400 g	new potatoes	14 oz
60 mL	walnut or sunflower oil	4 tbsp
1	small onion, sliced thickly	1
2	cloves garlic, finely chopped	2
3	small green chillies, seeded and finely chopped (if using dried chillies you will need to soak them in boiling water first)	3
50 g	broken walnuts	2 oz
50 g	crumbly white cheese (such as Lancashire or Caerphilly)	2 oz
200 g	cooked shrimps or prawns	7 oz
250 mL	milk	9 fl oz
	salt	

Steam or microwave the potatoes until cooked, then halve them lengthways. Meanwhile, heat the oil and gently fry the onion and garlic over a low heat until the onion is golden. Put the oil, onions, garlic, chillies, walnuts, cheese and half the shrimps or prawns in a food processor and purée, gradually adding the milk to reduce the consistency to a thick sauce. Add extra milk or oil if it seems too thick. Season to taste with salt.

While the potatoes are still warm, lay them out on a serving dish, pour the sauce over and decorate with the remaining shrimps or prawns.

The dish is best eaten when the potatoes are just warm but if you want to prepare it ahead of time and eat it cold, it is still excellent.

PER SERVING	
Energy Kcals	417.9
Protein g	18.47
Fat g	29.27
Saturated fatty acids g	5.58
Monounsaturated fatty acids g	6.83
Polyunsaturated fatty acids g	16.74
Carbohydrate g	21.68
Total Sugars g	6.00
Sodium mg	708.01
Fibre g	1.8

Since commercial salmon farming was introduced in the 1970s and 80s the price of salmon has plummeted so that it can now be eaten as an everyday dish.

Salmon Mousse with Green Peppercorns

Serves 8

A delicious dish for a summer evening with lots of fresh green salad. It needs to be made in advance so is a good dish for a party.

350 g	fresh salmon	12 oz
	juice of 2 lemons	
3	spring onions, chopped	3
250 mL	dry white wine	9 fl oz
250 mL	water	9 fl oz
2 tsp	green peppercorns in brine	2 tsp
250 mL	sour cream	9 fl oz
	salt	
15 g	gelatin	½ oz
4	egg whites	4

Put the salmon in a pan with half the lemon juice, spring onions, wine and water. Bring it to the boil and simmer it gently for 15 - 20 minutes or until the fish is flaking easily off the bone. Remove the fish (reserving the cooking liquid), bone and skin it.

Depending on whether you like your mousse chunky or smooth, mash the salmon with a fork or put it in a food processor. If you are going to process it, add the sour cream before you purée it; otherwise fold it into the mashed salmon.

Drain the peppercorns of their brine and mash them lightly with a fork then add them to the salmon.

Melt the gelatin in 120 mL / 4 fl oz of the cooking liquid, cool it back to room temperature and mix it into the mousse. Season the mixture to taste with salt and the remaining lemon juice, remembering that you will be adding egg whites which will slightly mute the taste. Put the mixture in the fridge until it is beginning to set.

Whisk the egg whites until they hold their shape and fold them into the mousse. Spoon it into a dish and return to the fridge to set fully. Decorate with a few lemon butterflies before serving with a cucumber salad and gluten-free brown bread and butter.

PER SERVING	
Energy Kcals	179.88
Protein g	12.85
Fat g	11.92
Saturated fatty acids g	5.2
Monounsaturated fatty acids g	4.37
Polyunsaturated fatty acids g	.01
Carbohydrate g	1.93
Total Sugars g	1.92
Sodium mg	193.91
Fibre g	.09

Eggs Florentine

Serves 4

A rather more substantial variation on a classic Eggs Florentine. You need to keep a close eye on the eggs while they cook as, depending on the accuracy of your oven and the size of the eggs, they may take more or less than the 15 minutes given.

45 mL	olive oil	3 tbsp
250 g	field mushrooms, sliced	9 oz
500 g	fresh spinach, well washed and dried	1 lb 2 oz
15 mL	pumpkin seeds	1 tbsp
4	large eggs	4
30 mL	Cheddar cheese, grated	2 tbsp
30 mL	Emmenthal cheese, grated	2 tbsp
75 mL	plain low fat yogurt (gluten-free)	5 tbsp
	salt	
	freshly ground black pepper	

Heat the oven to 170°C/325°F.

Heat the oil in a large pan and briskly cook the mushrooms for a couple of minutes. Add the spinach and let it wilt briefly, then mix in the pumpkin seeds and season lightly. Spoon the spinach into an ovenproof dish and make hollows for the eggs. Break in the eggs. Mix the cheeses and the yogurt together and spoon it over the eggs.

Bake for 15 minutes in a moderate oven (or 5 minutes in a microwave on High) or until the eggs are just set. Season, and serve at once.

PER SERVING	
Energy Kcals	352.03
Protein g	19.55
Fat g	28.5
Saturated fatty acids g	8.22
Monounsaturated fatty acids g	13.91
Polyunsaturated fatty acids g	4.39
Carbohydrate g	5.23
Total Sugars g	4.09
Sodium mg	501.9
Fibre g	3.64

As an alternative cocktail snack: do not roll the mixture flat but into little balls in your hands, then roll them in the sesame seeds. They will need to cook for a little longer as they will be thicker.

Cheese Sables

Delicious cheesey biscuits which can be used as a cocktail snack or with cheese. The quantities in this recipe will make approximately 20 cocktail-sized biscuits.

100 g	gram (chick pea) flour	4 oz
25 g	butter	1 oz
30 mL	strong Cheddar cheese, grated	2 tbsp
15 - 30 mL	water	1 - 2 tbsp
1	egg yolk	1
30 mL	sesame seeds (optional)	2 tbsp

Sieve the flour then cut in the butter. Rub in the butter with the cheese. Mix to a soft dough with the water then roll out on a well floured board. It will stick slightly but if you roll it with care and keep a spatula and some extra flour available it should be fine. Roll to a thickness of about 10 mm/^{1}/$_2$ inch then cut out with a small round cutter. Brush the top of each biscuit generously with the egg yolk and sprinkle with the sesame seeds. Place on an oiled baking tray.

Bake in a moderate oven (180°C/350°F) for 10 - 15 minutes until the biscuits are lightly tanned and crisp but take care that they do not burn. Cool on a rack before serving.

PER SERVING	
Energy Kcals	167.65
Protein g	6.76
Fat g	12.16
Saturated fatty acids g	5.07
Monounsaturated fatty acids g	3.69
Polyunsaturated fatty acids g	2.49
Carbohydrate g	8.42
Total Sugars g	.55
Sodium mg	91.67
Fibre g	2.31

Right:
Polenta with Gorgonzola
(page 22)

Herb and Bacon Casserole

Serves 6

This is based on a recipe for a medieval casserole which accounts for the large variety of herbs, as in the Middle Ages they were virtually interchangeable with vegetables.

75 g	rice flour, brown if possible	3 oz
75 g	chick pea (gram) flour	3 oz
75 g	butter or low-fat spread, suitable for baking	3 oz
350 g	bacon slices	12 oz
225 g	leeks, cleaned and sliced thickly	8 oz
225 g	fresh spinach, cleaned and roughly chopped	8 oz
1/2	container each mustard and cress	1/2
1	bunch watercress, stalks removed	1
1	handful fresh parsley	1
2	sprigs fresh thyme, stalks removed or 1 mL / 1/2 teaspoon dried	2
2	fresh sage leaves or 1 mL / 1/2 teaspoon dried	2
3	medium eggs	3
150 mL	chicken stock or water	5 fl oz
	black pepper	

Heat the oven to 180°C / 350°F .

Mix the flours together then rub in the fat until the mixture is the texture of breadcrumbs. Add enough cold water to make a firm dough and set aside.

Fry the bacon until crisp. Line a 20 cm (8 inch) quiche dish with half the bacon. Mix the leeks, spinach, cresses and herbs and pile them on the top of the bacon. Beat the eggs together, set aside a little egg with which to brush the top of the pie, then add the stock to the rest. Season with freshly ground black pepper (the bacon should be salty enough not to need any extra) and pour over the vegetables. Lay the remaining bacon over the vegetables.

On a well-floured (rice or chick pea) board roll out the pastry quite thickly. Place the pie dish on the pastry and cut out its shape. Use the trimmings to line the edge of the dish. Carefully lift the pastry on a rolling pin and cover the pie. Use the trimmings to

PER SERVING	
Energy Kcals	552.74
Protein g	21.5
Fat g	42.67
Saturated fatty acids g	14.92
Polyunsaturated fatty acids g	4.83
Monounsaturated fatty acids g	16.78
Carbohydrate g	21.28
Total Sugars g	2.88
Fibre g	3.79
Sodium mg	5141.08

Left:
French Toast (page 29)

decorate its top and brush with the reserved beaten egg.

Bake the pie for 30 - 40 minutes or until the pastry is crisp and golden. Serve warm rather than hot.

Crudités and Dips

Crudités are ideal for anyone with a gluten or wheat intolerance as the vegetables are all perfectly safe and it is easy to make dips which will also be wheat- and gluten-free. If you want to vary the textures, you can include potato or tortilla chips (that are gluten-free).

You will need up to 250 g / 9 oz of vegetables per person and around 100 g / 3 ½ oz of dip.

Ingredients:
Any raw vegetable, with the possible exception of potatoes, is good for crudités. Try to use contrasting colours and shapes on a general platter or restrict the vegetables to one or two colours for effect. Use:

Artichokes (Jerusalem) or globe leaves; **beans** - green, runner, French, etc. - raw or lightly cooked; **beets** - raw or lightly cooked; **broccoli florets** - raw or lightly cooked; **brussel sprouts** - raw or lightly cooked; **cabbage** - green, red, chinese leaves, etc. - raw; **carrots** - raw; **cauliflower florets** - raw or lightly cooked; **celery** - raw; **chicory** - raw; **courgettes** - raw; **baby corn** - raw; **cucumber**; **fennel** - raw or lightly cooked; **snow peas** - raw; **Chinese radish** - raw; **mushrooms** - raw; **parsnips** - raw; **peppers** - red, green, yellow, black - raw; **radishes**; **spring onions**; **cherry tomatoes**; **turnips** or anything else which appeals

Dips
Ready made taramasalata, hummus, tahini, raita - but check ingredients for wheat or gluten.

Start with gluten-free mayonnaise (bought or home-made but not salad cream), yogurt, sour cream, soft cream or cottage cheese.

Add: horseradish sauce, curry paste (check ingredients) and a little apricot jam, mustard of any kind (check ingredients), tomato purée or lots of chopped fresh herbs.

Season with: salt and pepper, lemon juice, Tabasco (a little), any chopped herb but try to avoid using dried herbs or spices as they tend to taste raw when they are not in a cooked dish.

It is not possible to give a nutritional analysis as the ingredients could be so different.

French toast is excellent just with bacon but you can make it into a more substantial dish by serving it with wheat/gluten-free sausages or, with jam or fruit jelly.

French Toast

Serves 6

French toast is normally one of those delicious dishes banned to those on a wheat- or gluten-free diet although it actually works very well with both home-made and bought wheat/gluten-free breads.

6	eggs	6
180 mL	milk	6 fl oz
½ tsp	ground cinnamon	½ tsp
50 g	poppy seeds	2 oz
	salt and pepper	
350 g	lean bacon slices	12 oz
6	large thick slices of wheat- and gluten-free bread - see page 189	6
25g	butter	1 oz
45 mL	olive oil	3 tbsp

Whisk the eggs with the milk, cinnamon and poppy seeds in a large flattish dish. Season it with pepper only. Submerge the slices of bread in the mixture and, if you have time, leave them to soak for half an hour.

To cook, fry the bacon in its own fat until it is tanned but not burned. Remove with a slotted spoon and drain on a piece of paper towel and keep it warm. Tip the bacon fat into a large, clean frying pan with the butter or olive oil and heat gently. With a spatula, transfer the bread slices to the pan and fry them gently on both sides until they are lightly browned and slightly puffed. Serve them at once with the bacon.

PER SERVING	
Energy Kcals	542.46
Protein g	22.4
Fat g	40.55
Saturated fatty acids g	14.8
Monounsaturated fatty acids g	16.46
Polyunsaturated fatty acids g	5.61
Carbohydrate g	24.21
Total Sugars g	3.87
Sodium mg	1293.37
Fibre g	2.41

Puff and flaky pastry are difficult for any cook to make so if you succeed with a wheat/gluten-free pastry, you can count yourself a real pastry chef!

Vol Au Vent Cases

Serves 8

These vol au vent cases can be filled with any filling (see pancake filling on page 127 or smoked salmon mousse on page 24) of your choice and served either hot or cold.

150 g	sifted gram (chick pea) flour	5 oz
	pinch of salt	
125 g	butter	4 oz
	water	

Sift the flour into a bowl with the salt. Cut the butter into walnut-size pieces and mix it into the flour in lumps. Add approximately 60 mL / 4 tablespoons of chilled water to make a firmish dough. Put it to chill in a plastic bag in the fridge for 15 minutes.

On a floured board lay out the pastry. Working as for puff pastry (bring the rolling pin down quite heavily on the pastry and then give it a quick roll backwards and forwards - do not push as with ordinary pastry or the butter will be moved out of place), roll to a strip about 15 cm (6 inches) long and 5 cm (2 inches) thick. Fold in three, turn around so that the open edge is facing you and roll again, this time to around 3 cm (1½ inch) in thickness. Fold in three and set aside to cool again for 15 minutes. Repeat this process twice more.

To make the cases heat the oven to 180°C / 350°F.

Roll the pastry out again (this amount of pastry will make 8 medium-sized vol au vents or 12 cocktail size) to around 3 cm (1½ inch) thickness. Use a pastry cutter or a glass to cut out 8 rounds. Then use a small cutter or glass to make 8 small circles inside the cases but take care not to go right through the pastry.

Place on a greased baking tray and cook for 10 - 15 minutes until the pastry is slightly risen, tanned and crisp.

Remove carefully to a rack and, with a sharp knife, remove each "lid" from the centre of the vol au vent. Remove any uncooked dough from the inside and replace the lid.

PER SERVING	
Energy Kcals	173.84
Protein g	3.77
Fat g	13.78
Saturated fatty acids g	8.53
Monounsaturated fatty acids g	3.3
Polyunsaturated fatty acids g	.91
Carbohydrate g	9.46
Total Sugars g	.64
Sodium mg	148.78
Fibre g	2.01

Fish

Salmon Koulibiac

Poached Fish with Rice

Persian Squid Pilaf

Tuna Curry with Coconut and Coriander

Smoked Mackerel and Parsnip Bake

Salmon, Apple and Peanut Salad

Salmon en Papillotte

Edward Abbott's Shellfish Salad

Dutch Herring and Beet Salad

Fish Crumble

Guyanan Okra with Prawns

Crab Casserole

Ever Popular Fish Cakes

Paella

Stir Fried Artichokes with Tuna

Salmon Koulibiac

Serves 6

This classic Russian recipe makes a great dish for a dinner party or a buffet. It looks impressive, is pretty filling - but not expensive to make.

300 g	fresh salmon, fillet or cutlets	10 oz
2	slices of lemon	2
200 g	brown rice	7 oz
200 g	sifted gram (chick pea) flour	7 oz
100 g	butter	4 oz
15 mL	olive oil	1 tbsp
1	medium onion, finely chopped	1
50 g	mushrooms, finely chopped	2 oz
	large handful of fresh parsley, chopped	
	juice of 2 lemons	
2	eggs	2
5 mL or less	salt	small tsp
	black pepper	

Heat the oven to 180°C / 350°F.

Put the salmon in a flat pan with the lemon slices. Cover with water, bring slowly to the boil and simmer for 8 - 10 minutes or until it is cooked through.

Remove the fish and set it aside, discard the lemon slices and add the rice to the water. Bring back to the boil and boil briskly for 15 minutes or until the rice is cooked. Add more water if it looks as though it is drying out.

Rub the butter into the flour, then mix to a soft dough with a couple of tablespoons of water. Take 1/3 of the dough and roll it out into a circle slightly less than 1 cm (1/2 inch) thick and put it on a greased baking tray. Do not worry if the pastry crumbles somewhat, just stick it back together with a little water. Bake this pastry "plate" in the oven for 15 minutes or until it is crisp.

Meanwhile, heat the oil in a heavy pan and add the onion and mushrooms. Cook together gently for 5 - 8 minutes or until they are cooked through.

When the rice is cooked, drain it and put it into a bowl and add the onion and mushroom mixture. Flake in the salmon, then add

PER SERVING	
Energy Kcals	499.58
Protein g	21.21
Fat g	27.36
Saturated fatty acids g	11.85
Monounsaturated fatty acids g	9.62
Polyunsaturated fatty acids g	4.13
Carbohydrate g	45.89
Total Sugars g	3.14
Sodium mg	542.58
Fibre g	4.75

the parsley, lemon juice, salt and pepper. Beat the eggs in a bowl and add most of them, reserving a little to paint the outside of the Koulibiac. Mix it all together thoroughly.

Pile the rice and fish mixture on top of the cooked pastry. Roll out the remains of the pastry and cover the rice mixture with it, pressing down the edges to make a seal. Once again, do not worry if it falls apart on you. Just patch it and then paint generously with the reserved egg. You can also use the pastry trimmings to decorate the Koulibiac.

Return to the oven for another 20 minutes or until the pastry is cooked and lightly browned.

Serve hot with a moist vegetable such as a ratatouille or cold (at room temperature) with a salad.

Poached Fish with Rice appeared on every grand Edwardian breakfast table along with the kidneys and bacon and the cold roasts from the night before. It then graduated to a brunch dish and has now come full circle and is served in smart restaurants as a lunch or supper dish.

Poached Fish with Rice

Serves 6

The classic fish dish from the Indian empire. Being rice based it is fine for those on wheat- or gluten-free diets but check that the curry powder does not contain wheat starch.

350 g	smoked haddock fillets or salmon	12 oz
180 g	long grain rice	6 oz
1	small onion	1
25 g	butter	1 oz
75 g	raisins	3 oz
10 mL	wheat- and gluten-free curry powder	2 tsp
45 mL	olive oil	3 tbsp
1	hard-boiled egg	1
	juice of 1 lemon	

Poach the fish for 10 minutes in gently boiling water. At the same time cook the rice in boiling water for approximately 10 minutes or until it is just cooked. Chop the onion finely and fry it gently in the butter until it is soft but not coloured.

While the onion and rice are cooking, pour boiling water over the raisins and soak them for 10 minutes.

Drain and flake the fish; drain and rinse the rice in boiling water and drain the raisins. Set all on one side to be amalgamated into the final dish.

In a double boiler or an ovenproof dish with a lid, put the fried onion in the bottom and cover it with the raisins and then with the flaked fish. Heat the oil and mix it with the curry powder to make a paste. Mix this into the rice and spoon the rice over the fish.

Cover the dish with a tea towel and then with a lid so that it is well sealed. If in a double boiler, simmer for 25 minutes; if in a casserole, cook in a slow oven (150°C/ 300°F) for 25 minutes.

To serve, heat a flat dish and turn the kedgeree out onto it so that the fish, raisins, etc. are uppermost. Finely chop the hard-boiled egg, sprinkle it over the top and pour over the lemon juice. Serve at once.

PER SERVING	
Energy Kcals	307.37
Protein g	15.11
Fat g	12.67
Saturated fatty acids g	3.89
Monounsaturated fatty acids g	6.81
Polyunsaturated fatty acids g	1.30
Carbohydrate g	33.94
Total Sugars g	9.96
Sodium mg	497.38
Fibre g	.47

Anyone who feels squeamish about squid (and many people do) could substitute prawns for the squid in this recipe and it would taste just as good.

Persian Squid Pilaf

Serves 6

If you can get the ink from the squid you can turn this into an even more exotic dish by adding the ink to the cooking liquid - and turning the whole dish black!

75 mL	olive oil	5 tbsp
1	medium onion, peeled and chopped finely	1
2	large yellow peppers	2
2	cloves garlic, finely chopped	2
250 g	Patna (long-grain) rice	9 oz
5 mL	ground allspice	1 tsp
5 mL	ground cumin	1 tsp
10 mL	dried mint	2 tsp
200 g	prepared squid , fresh or frozen, sliced	7 oz
50 g	currants	2 oz
	salt	
	pepper	
	juice 2 large lemons	
	large handful of fresh coriander, chopped	

Heat the oil in a large, flat pan and gently cook the onion, peppers and garlic until they are soft but not browned. Add the rice, spices and herbs and stir for a few minutes, then add enough water to cover the rice. Bring the mixture to the boil and simmer, with the pan uncovered, for 10 - 15 minutes or until the rice is just cooked but not mushy. (You may have to add a little extra water if it dries up too fast.) Add the squid, currants and seasoning to taste. Cook for a couple more minutes, then add the lemon juice and coriander. Serve warm or cold with a green salad.

PER SERVING	
Energy Kcals	333.00
Protein g	9.15
Fat g	13.63
Saturated fatty acids g	2.70
Monounsaturated fatty acids g	9.70
Polyunsaturated fatty acids g	1.62
Carbohydrate g	44.29
Total Sugars g	10.65
Sodium mg	133.14
Fibre g	1.60

This curry (without the coriander leaves) even finds favour with children who normally adore tuna but are not so keen on curry sauces.

Tuna Curry with Coconut and Coriander

Serves 6

If you do not like coriander leaves, substitute flat-leaved French parsley.

3	tins (200 g) of tuna in oil	3
2	leeks, trimmed and sliced thinly	2
2 cm	cube of ginger root, peeled and finely sliced	1 inch
5	large cloves garlic, peeled and sliced	5
1	small green chilli, seeded and finely sliced	1
2	medium green peppers, seeded and sliced	2
45 mL	medium curry powder - check the ingredients to make sure there is no wheat or gluten	3 tbsp
1.5	tins (400 g) of chick peas, drained	1 1/2
1.5	tins (400 g) of coconut milk	1 1/2
	juice of 2 - 3 limes or lemons	
2	handfuls of coriander leaves, chopped	2

Drain the oil from the tuna into a heavy wide pan. Add the leeks, ginger root, garlic, chilli, green pepper and curry powder and cook them all together for 3 - 4 minutes.

Add the chick peas and coconut milk, bring to the boil and simmer covered for a further 10 minutes. Add the tuna fish and cook for a further 5 minutes.

Finally add the lime or lemon juice to taste and seasoning if it is needed.

Serve the curry, liberally sprinkled with the fresh coriander, with lots of freshly cooked rice and a green salad.

PER SERVING	
Energy Kcals	337.38
Protein g	35.17
Fat g	12.54
Saturated fatty acids g	1.95
Monounsaturated fatty acids g	4.66
Polyunsaturated fatty acids g	6.80
Carbohydrate g	22.66
Total Sugars g	7.35
Sodium mg	605.45
Fibre g	7.08

Mackerel is one of those oily fish high in Omega 3 fatty acids which health experts are so keen that we should eat.

Smoked Mackerel and Parsnip Bake

Serves 4

This is a very simple pie to make and very flavoursome. If you cannot get parsnips or celeriac, you can substitute any other flavourful root vegetable. To make the pie more "child friendly" you could also exchange the artichoke hearts for tinned corn and leave out the olives!

500 g	parsnips, scrubbed and sliced	1lb 2oz
500 g	celeriac, scrubbed, trimmed and diced	1lb 2oz
2	large fillets of smoked mackerel	2
300 g	fresh tomatoes, sliced	10 oz
200 g	tinned artichoke hearts, drained and sliced	7 oz
50 g	black olives, pitted and halved	2 oz
1	pack plain potato chips (gluten free), crushed	1
45 mL, hpd	sesame seeds	1 hpd tbsp

Steam the parsnips and celeriac until soft. Mash them roughly, season them to taste and spoon them into the bottom of a casserole or pie dish.

Skin and remove any bones from the mackerel and flake it over the vegetables. Cover the mackerel with the sliced tomatoes and artichoke hearts, and then the halved olives. Mix the chips with the sesame seeds and sprinkle over the tomatoes and olives. Bake the casserole in a moderate oven (180°C/350°F) for 30 minutes or until all is thoroughly warmed through and the top is crisp.

PER SERVING	
Energy Kcals	483.43
Protein g	20.95
Fat g	33.87
Saturated fatty acids g	7.08
Monounsaturated fatty acids g	15.77
Polyunsaturated fatty acids g	8.44
Carbohydrate g	25.32
Total Sugars g	12.21
Sodium mg	1061.5
Fibre g	12.45

It is surprising how well fruit goes with fish, both cooked and raw. Classic combinations such as mackerel and gooseberry, and salmon with apple, use the sharpness of the fruit to counteract the richness of the oily fish.

Salmon, Apple and Peanut Salad

Serves 4

A very quick and easy salad to make - it is given great texture by the combination of crunchy apple and peanut with the softness of the salmon.

1	tin (400 g) red salmon	1
2	medium-sized Granny Smith apples	2
100 g	peanuts	4 oz
120 mL	home made or good-quality bought mayonnaise (check the ingredients list for wheat starch / gluten)	4 fl oz
	juice of ½ a large lemon	
	pinch of salt	
	freshly ground black pepper	
	iceberg lettuce	

Drain the salmon and flake it. Core and dice the apples but do not peel them. Mix the salmon in with the apples and peanuts. Thin the mayonnaise with the lemon juice and season to taste with salt and pepper. Toss the fish and apple mixture in the mayonnaise and adjust the seasoning to taste.

Arrange the lettuce on a serving dish and pile the fish mixture on the top to serve.

PER SERVING	
Energy Kcals	503.48
Protein g	24.94
Fat g	41.40
Saturated fatty acids g	7.51
Monounsaturated fatty acids g	24.9
Polyunsaturated fatty acids g	8.33
Carbohydrate g	8.48
Total Sugars g	6.83
Sodium mg	698.31
Fibre g	2.51

Barbecue cooking is excellent for people with food allergies as long as they make sure that what they eat is cooked without any dressing apart from a little oil or salt and pepper. They can then easily take their own small pot of dressing to spice up their barbecue.

Salmon en Papillotte

Serves 6

This dish started life at dinner parties in Victorian India where it could be made with any white fish and must have been very light and refreshing when compared to the heavy English fare that so many expatriots favoured. If you prefer, you can substitute fillets of hake or halibut for the salmon.

6	salmon steaks	6
90 mL	olive or walnut oil	6 tbsp
50 g	finely chopped shallots	2 oz
2	cloves garlic, finely chopped	2
	large handful of fresh parsley	
45 mL	white wine vinegar	3 tbsp
	grated peel of 2 limes	
	pinch salt	
	pepper	

Put the fish in a microwave dish or flattish pan, cover it with boiling water and simmer for 5 minutes on the stove or 2 minutes in a microwave. Drain carefully and set side. Mix all the other ingredients thoroughly in a glass or porcelain dish large enough to hold the fish comfortably. Lay the fish on top of the marinade, then spoon over the excess to make sure the steaks are well immersed. Cover the dish and leave for 6 - 12 hours.

To cook the fish, lay the cutlets, with their marinade, in an ample bed of foil and cover them with well-oiled greaseproof paper. The fish can then be cooked on a barbecue, under a hot grill or in a wide heavy frying pan. It should take between 6 and 8 minutes, depending on the thickness of the steaks.

Serve with their marinade juices and lots of white rice and lightly cooked snow peas.

PER SERVING	
Energy Kcals	216.75
Protein g	8.21
Fat g	20.06
Saturated fatty acids g	3.10
Monounsaturated fatty acids g	12.69
Polyunsaturated fatty acids g	3.11
Carbohydrate g	1.07
Total Sugars g	.62
Sodium mg	173.52
Fibre g	.35

The mashed potato base for this recipe makes an excellent dish on its own. You could use it as a vegetable with a meat dish or salad, either hot or cold, or try serving it hot with bacon, or a poached egg perched on the top.

Edward Abbott's Shellfish Salad

Serves 6

Another fish dish from the outposts of the Victorian British Empire. This one comes from Edward Abbott - a very well-travelled Tasmanian gourmet whose fascinating cookbook included lamb cooked with 500 g of garlic cloves, as well as this salad.

450 g	mashing potatoes	1 lb
6	hard-boiled egg yolks	6
60 mL	white wine vinegar	4 tbsp
8 tbsp	olive oil	8 tbsp
4 tsp	wholegrain mustard (check ingredients to make sure it does not contain gluten/wheat)	4 tsp
	salt	
½ tsp	cayenne pepper	½ tsp
60 mL	milk	4 tbsp
6	whole scallops	6
200 g	crab meat	7 oz
100 g	cooked squid, fresh or frozen	4 oz
1	largish head crisp lettuce	1
6	king prawns, fresh cooked or frozen	6
1	bunch watercress	1

Scrub and boil, or steam, the potatoes in their skins. Cool them slightly, then skin them and mash with the hard-boiled egg yolks. Add the vinegar, olive oil, mustard, salt and cayenne, then reduce the purée with the milk and amalgamate the mixture thoroughly. Simmer the scallops in a little white wine or water with a slice of lemon for 4 - 5 minutes or until they are cooked through. Set aside to cool.

Mix the crabmeat and squid into the potato and adjust the seasoning to taste. Allow to cool completely. To serve, make a bed of lettuce on the serving dish. Pile the potato and fish mixture in the middle and garnish with the scallops, king prawns and the watercress.

PER SERVING	
Energy Kcals	458.78
Protein g	31.61
Fat g	30.60
Saturated fatty acids g	6.43
Monounsaturated fatty acids g	19.12
Polyunsaturated fatty acids g	3.95
Carbohydrate g	15.96
Total Sugars g	2.83
Sodium mg	760.67
Fibre g	1.71

Fresh beet is a greatly under-rated vegetable. It is deliciously flavoured and would be excellent for pregnant mothers as it is high in folate as well as fibre. Steam small beets until just cooked, then serve them with butter or olive oil and freshly grated sea salt.

Dutch Herring and Beet Salad

Serves 6

This salad has a real Nordic flavour of the sea. Great for summer lunches or picnics.

250 g	baby beets, scrubbed	9 oz
250 g	new potatoes, scrubbed	9 oz
4	ready pickled herrings	4
225 mL	plain low-fat yogurt, gluten free	8 fl oz
	large handful of chopped fresh parsley	
	juice of 1 large lemon	
	salt	
	pepper	

Steam the beets and potatoes until cooked, then cut the beets into matchsticks and cut the potatoes into slices. Unroll the pickled herrings, flatten them out and cut them into thin match sticks.

Mix the fish, beets and potatoes in a bowl, then add the yogurt and parsley and mix together until the fish and vegetables are thoroughly coated in the yogurt. Season to taste with the lemon juice, salt and pepper and serve with lots of fresh wheat- and gluten-free brown bread.

PER SERVING	
Energy Kcals	194.95
Protein g	13.57
Fat g	7.86
Saturated fatty acids g	.64
Monounsaturated fatty acids g	.97
Polyunsaturated fatty acids g	.35
Carbohydrate g	18.06
Total Sugars g	11.63
Sodium mg	665.55
Fibre g	1.43

If you like a crunchy consistency to a crumble topping, you can always spread some crushed gluten-free potato chips over the top and brown them lightly under a broiler just before serving.

Fish Crumble

Serves 4

This simple fish crumble should appeal to adults and children alike - although you might want to leave the prawns out of the children's version.

450 g	haddock fillets	1 lb
1	largish onion, chopped roughly	1
225 g	leeks, trimmed and sliced thickly	8 oz
450 mL	milk	16 fl oz
15 mL	butter or low-fat spread	1 tbsp
15 mL	potato flour	1 tbsp
100 g	fresh or frozen prawns	4 oz
	salt and pepper	
75 g	rice flour	3 oz
25 g	corn flour or cornmeal	1 oz
50 g	butter or low-fat spread	2 oz
50 g	strong flavoured cheese, grated	2 oz

Heat the oven to 180°C/ 350°F.

Put the fish, with the onion, leeks and milk into a pan or a microwave dish. Cover and cook on the stove for 10 - 15 minutes, in a microwave on high for 8 minutes or until the fish flakes easily.

Remove the fish carefully from the pan, get rid of any skin or bones and flake the flesh coarsely. Strain the milk, setting it aside and reserving the onions and leeks. Melt the butter or spread in a clean pan (it will stick if you use the milky one), and add the potato flour. Mix well, then slowly add the milk, stirring continually and cook until the sauce thickens. Add the haddock, prawns and vegetables and seasoning to taste; spoon into an ovenproof casserole or pie dish.

Rub the butter or low-fat spread and grated cheese into the flours until you have a crumble consistency, then spread it over the fish mixture. Bake for 30 minutes to cook and brown the crumble. Serve at once with a couple of green vegetables.

PER SERVING	
Energy Kcals	414.99
Protein g	23.13
Fat g	21.93
Saturated fatty acids g	9.48
Monounsaturated fatty acids g	8.39
Polyunsaturated fatty acids g	2.98
Carbohydrate g	25.94
Total Sugars g	5.48
Sodium mg	774.46
Fibre g	2.55

Okra is very popular in Caribbean cooking and adds a delicious subtle flavour to a sauce. However, you need to make sure that it is well cooked to get the best from it. It is not a vegetable that is improved by being served *al dente*.

Guyanan Okra with Prawns

Serves 4

The idea for this recipe was given to me by Rosamund Grant whose Afro-Caribbean cooking books have made Caribbean cooking come alive for me.

60 mL	sunflower oil	4 tbsp
1	medium onion, chopped	1
1	large clove garlic, chopped	1
200 g	okra, topped, tailed and chopped	7 oz
1/2	small green pepper, seeded and sliced	1/2
2.5 mL	paprika	1/2 tsp
2.5 mL	ground cumin	1/2 tsp
15 mL	chopped fresh parsley	1 tbsp
250 g	fresh or frozen (thawed) prawns	9 oz
	salt	
	pepper	
2	medium-sized tomatoes, chopped	2

Cook the onion and garlic in the oil for a few minutes, then add the okra and the pepper and continue to cook for 7 - 10 minutes. Add the spices, herbs, prawns and a little seasoning and go on cooking for a further 10 - 15 minutes. Finally add the tomatoes, stir well, adjust the seasoning to taste and cook for a further minute or two to get the tomatoes well warmed through. Serve with boiled brown or white rice.

PER SERVING	
Energy Kcals	222.5
Protein g	14.11
Fat g	16.26
Saturated fatty acids g	2.33
Monounsaturated fatty acids g	3.83
Polyunsaturated fatty acids g	9.89
Carbohydrate g	5.71
Total Sugars g	4.55
Sodium mg	596.17
Fibre g	3.43

Frozen or even tinned crabmeat work very well for this dish if you cannot get fresh.

Crab Casserole

Serves 6

This is a delicious dish for anyone who enjoys crabmeat - but does not like having to struggle with the shell! It also reheats well.

30 mL	olive oil	2 tbsp
100 g	leeks, cleaned and very finely sliced	4 oz
100 g	fennel , cleaned and very finely sliced	4 oz
100 g	mushrooms, chopped	4 oz
15 mL	corn starch	1 tbsp
150 mL	milk	5 fl oz
400 g	cooked crabmeat, brown and white mixed	14oz
30 mL	fresh sour cream (gluten-free)	2 tbsp
	juice of 1 lemon	
150 mL	medium sherry (optional)	5 fl oz
75 g	rice flour	3 oz
75 g	gram (chick pea) flour	3 oz
30 mL, hpd	wheat- and gluten-free baking powder	2 hpd tsp
50 g	butter	2 oz
30 mL	freshly grated Parmesan	2 tbsp
200 mL	buttermilk or soured milk	7 fl oz
	sea salt	
	freshly ground black pepper	

Heat the oven to 180°C/ 350°F.

   Heat the oil in a heavy pan and add the leeks and fennel. Cover and turn heat down really low; sweat vegetables for 15 - 20 minutes or until they are really soft. Add the mushrooms and continue to cook for a further 5 minutes. Add the corn starch, stir a minute or two, then gradually add all the milk, stirring while the sauce thickens. Add the crabmeat, sour cream, lemon juice and sherry and season to taste. Pour the mixture into an ovenproof casserole or pie dish.

   Meanwhile, mix the flours with the baking powder and rub in the butter. Add the Parmesan, then stir in the soured milk (if you cannot get sour milk squeeze a little lemon juice into the fresh milk) until it reaches a soft dropping consistency.

PER SERVING	
Energy Kcals	414.99
Protein g	23.13
Fat g	21.93
Saturated fatty acids g	9.48
Monounsaturated fatty acids g	8.39
Polyunsaturated fatty acids g	2.98
Carbohydrate g	25.94
Total Sugars g	5.48
Sodium mg	774.46
Fibre g	2.55

Spoon the scone mixture over the crab - it does not matter if it is not smooth - and bake in the oven for 30 - 35 minutes until the top is crisp and lightly tanned.

Serve the fish cakes to the whole family so that everyone gets used to eating more wheat-free food. The chances are that they will not notice any difference!

Ever Popular Fish Cakes

Serves 4

If your children prefer fish fingers, these cakes can just as eaily be made into a finger shape.

400 g	cod or haddock fillets	14 oz
200 g	mashing potatoes, scrubbed or peeled	7 oz
45 mL	milk	3 tbsp
5 mL	butter	1 tsp
	salt	
	black pepper	
	juice of 1 lemon	
1 package	plain potato chips, gluten free, crushed very finely	1 package
15 mL	sunflower oil	1 tbsp

Steam, boil or microwave the potatoes until they are well cooked, then skin and mash them with the milk, butter and a little seasoning.

Bring the fish, just covered in water, to the boil in a microwave or in a pan and simmer for 4 - 5 minutes or until it is cooked. Remove from the water and flake or, if you like your fish cakes very smooth, purée in a food processor. Mix the fish thoroughly into the potato and adjust the seasoning to taste.

Form the mixture into four large fish cakes and cover them thoroughly with the potato chips. Heat the oil in a wide pan and gently fry the fish cakes for about 8 minutes on each side or until they are nicely crisped.

They can be served alone or with a tomato sauce or gluten- and wheat-free ketchup.

PER SERVING	
Energy Kcals	234.28
Protein g	20.53
Fat g	9.34
Saturated fatty acids g	3.53
Monounsaturated fatty acids g	2.40
Polyunsaturated fatty acids g	2.98
Carbohydrate g	18.58
Total Sugars g	1.30
Sodium mg	217.05
Fibre g	1.52

Mussels are greatly under-rated as a food, which is a pity as they are so quick and easy to cook, quite cheap and many would say taste just as good as much more expensive oysters.

Paella

Serves 6

A classic Spanish dish - and excellent for those on a wheat- or gluten-free diet as neither wheat not gluten has any place in it. It looks rather long and complicated but really is not - and well worth the little extra effort.

500 g	fresh mussels in their shells. You can also use 200 g/7 oz frozen mussels off their shells although the flavour will not be quite as good	1 lb 2 oz
500 g	large prawns or crayfish, fresh if possible but if not, frozen	1 lb 2 oz
60 mL	olive oil	4 tbsp
1	medium onion, chopped finely	1
2	cloves garlic, chopped finely	2
1	large green pepper, seeded and chopped	1
1	large tomato	1
5 mL	paprika	1 tsp
6 5 mL	saffron threads **or** ground saffron	6 1 tsp
	a few drops of Tabasco	
100 g	chorizo sausage, cut in thickish slices	4 oz
250 g	monkfish fillets, cut into cubes	9 oz
500 g	short-grained brown or Arborio rice	1 lb 2 oz
1.3 L	water	2¼ pints
	salt	
2	handfuls of fresh parsley, chopped	2
250 g	fresh young peas, podded, or frozen petits pois	9 oz

Scrub the mussels thoroughly and remove any beards. Heat 5 cm/ 2 inches of water in a large pan, then throw in the mussels and let them steam for 5 - 6 minutes. Discard any that have not opened and set the rest aside, reserving the juices.

If you are using fresh crayfish or prawns, boil them in 10 cm/ 4 inches of lightly salted water for 6 minutes, then leave to cool in the water. Shell the fish and reserve the water.

Heat the oil in a wide heavy pan and gently fry the onion, garlic and pepper until they are soft but not coloured. Chop the tomato into small pieces and add it to the pan. Continue to cook until the tomato has reduced. Stir in the paprika, saffron and Tabasco. Add the juices from the mussels and prawns and the chorizo sausage. Finally add the monkfish cubes, the rice, and the peas if you are using fresh. Pour in enough boiling water to cover the rice then bring the paella back to the boil and simmer gently, uncovered, for 15 - 20 minutes or until the rice is cooked. Add more water if it looks as though it is drying up.

When the rice is done, add the shellfish (either the pre-cooked fresh or the frozen - defrosted), the frozen peas (if you are using frozen rather than fresh) and the parsley. Cover the dish loosely and leave to rest for 15 minutes. Adjust the seasoning before serving.

PER SERVING	
Energy Kcals	658.98
Protein g	43.75
Fat g	18.88
Saturated fatty acids g	4.24
Monounsaturated fatty acids g	10.52
Polyunsaturated fatty acids g	2.75
Carbohydrate g	78.3
Total Sugars g	5.39
Sodium mg	1065.23
Fibre g	3.29

Stir fries are a wonderful way of creating a tasty supper from left-over vegetables. Quick and easy to cook, you can add flavour and nutrients with a few nuts or seeds added at the last moment.

Stir Fried Artichokes with Tuna

Serves 4

A quick and spicy dish with a distinctly Chinese flavour. However, take care if you want to use any of the standard Chinese sauces (soy, hoisin, yellow bean, etc.) as most of them contain wheat starch.

45 mL	olive oil	3 tbsp
3	fresh green chillies, carefully seeded and finely sliced	3
3	large cloves garlic, peeled and thinly sliced	3
6	spring onions, trimmed and chopped	6
150 g	fennel, trimmed and cut into matchsticks	5 oz
400 g	Jerusalem artichokes scrubbed and cut into matchsticks	14 oz
1	tin (400 g) tuna, drained and flaked	1
30 mL	sunflower seeds	2 tbsp
2 tbsp	gluten-free soya sauce	2 tbsp
	black pepper	
	fresh parsley, roughly chopped	

Heat the oil in a wide pan or wok and cook the chillies, garlic and spring onions until they are lightly coloured. Add the artichoke and fennel matchsticks and stir well for a couple of minutes. Add the tuna, well broken up, and the sunflower seeds. Cook uncovered for a minute or two, then reduce the heat, cover the pan and cook gently or sweat for around 15 minutes or until the artichoke is just cooked but still crisp. Add the gluten-free soya sauce and stir well to amagalmate - season with pepper. Add the parsley and serve at once with plenty of brown rice or wheat- and gluten-free noodles.

PER SERVING	
Energy Kcals	400.16
Protein g	27.77
Fat g	25.60
Saturated fatty acids g	4.71
Polyunsaturated fatty acids g	10.74
Monounsaturated fatty acids g	12.47
Carbohydrate g	17.42
Total Sugars g	3.50
Sodium mg	658.91
Fibre g	6.41

Pasta

Fresh Pasta

Red Pepper and Chicken Pasta Casserole

Seafood Pasta

Sunflower and Coriander Pesto

Curried Pasta Casserole

Basic Tomato Sauce

Lasagne

Spaghetti with Smoked Salmon

Penne with Frankfurters and Spring Greens

Pasta Primavera

Avocado and Bacon Salad

Spaghetti Bolognese

Pasta and Broccoli au Gratin

Pasta Rusticano

Tuna and Corn Macaroni

Frankfurter and Cheese Ravioli

*Vegan Pasta with Spinach
and Broad Beans*

Proprietary wheat- and gluten-free pastas can be excellent - we find that the rice ones work especially well - but they are expensive and not always easy to find. Since they come dried it would be worth keeping a stock in the fridge for the day when you do not have the time or energy to make your own.

Fresh Pasta

Serves 4

If you cannot buy wheat- and gluten-free ready-made pasta, you will have to make your own. If you have an electric pasta maker this is very easy but electric pasta makers are quite expensive. However, even if you do not want to invest a lot of money, it would be worth buying a hand pasta maker which will at least save you the rolling and cutting which used to take up so much of the average Italian housewife's time.

200 g	sifted chick pea (gram) flour	7 oz
50 g	rice flour	2 oz
2	medium eggs	2

If you have an electric pasta maker, put in the flours, then add the eggs according to the instructions. This mixture will work for spaghetti, tagliatelli, penne and lasagne sheets.

If you have a hand pasta maker, sift the flours together, make a well in the centre, break in the eggs and gradually draw them into the flour and mix to a soft dough. Then feed the mixture through the pasta maker according to its instructions.

Leave the pasta to "rest" for at least 30 minutes, then cook in plenty of lightly salted boiling water for 4 - 6 minutes depending on which shape and thickness of pasta you have made and serve with the sauce of your choice.

PER SERVING	
Energy Kcals	246.35
Protein g	14.40
Fat g	6.04
Saturated fatty acids g	1.18
Monounsaturated fatty acids g	1.96
Polyunsaturated fatty acids g	1.71
Carbohydrate g	35.11
Total Sugars g	1.60
Sodium mg	62.13
Fibre g	5.60

Raw red peppers are immensely popular with children as a snack - and brimming with nutrients and vitamins. To tempt them first time round, cut the peppers in thin slices and mix them in with some yellow and a few green pepper slices. I have never known it to fail!

Red Pepper and Chicken Pasta Casserole

Serves 4

A cheerful and filling casserole which will go down well with children and adults alike.

45 mL	olive oil	3 tbsp
2	cloves garlic, finely chopped	2
1	large red pepper, seeded and finely sliced	1
200 g	cooked chicken, chopped small	7 oz
10 mL	dried oregano	2 tsp
	salt	
	pepper	
300 mL	dry white wine or chicken stock	10 fl oz
100 g	Greek yogurt, gluten free	4 oz
250 g	gluten- and wheat-free pasta shapes (see page 202 or use a commercial brand)	9 oz
50 g	grated Parmesan cheese	2 oz
1	small pack plain potato chips (gluten free), crushed with a rolling pin	1

Heat the oil in a heavy pan and gently fry the garlic and pepper for a few minutes. Add the chicken, oregano and wine. Cover and simmer for 10 minutes. Add the yogurt and stir in well. Adjust the seasoning to taste.

Meanwhile cook the pasta according to the instructions on the pack.

Put a layer of the filling in the bottom of a heat-proof dish. Cover this with the pasta and cover the pasta with the remaining filling. Sprinkle the grated cheese and crushed potato chips generously over the top and brown lightly under a hot broiler for a few minutes. Serve at once.

PER SERVING	
Energy Kcals	586.95
Protein g	30.28
Fat g	23.34
Saturated fatty acids g	6.82
Monounsaturated fatty acids g	11.84
Polyunsaturated fatty acids g	3.16
Carbohydrate g	55.85
Total Sugars g	5.59
Sodium mg	373.60
Fibre g	3.21

For those people worried about their fat levels and too much cream, soya milk manufacturers now make excellent soya creams which can be happily substituted for real cream in cooked dishes.

Seafood Pasta

Serves 4

This is a rather spectacular dish but it needs good organization as you must cook all three parts of the dish at the same time and serve it as soon as it is cooked to do it full justice.

300 g	wheat- and gluten-free noodles. See page 202 or buy a commercial brand. However, depending on which variety you use you may need slightly more or slightly less as some "bulk up" more than others.	10 ½ oz
100 g	leeks, trimmed and finely sliced	4 oz
1	red chilli, seeded and finely sliced	1
30 mL	olive oil	2 tbsp
1 kg	fresh mussels in their shells	2 lb 4 oz
300 mL	dry white wine	10 fl oz
	generous handful of parsley, finely chopped	
100 g	cockles, fresh or frozen but very well rinsed	4 oz
15 mL	brandy	1 tbsp
100 mL	whipping cream	4 fl oz
	salt	
	pepper	

PER SERVING	
Energy Kcals	722.55
Protein g	43.07
Fat g	27.74
Saturated fatty acids g	8.88
Monounsaturated fatty acids g	9.63
Polyunsaturated fatty acids g	2.76
Carbohydrate g	65.67
Total Sugars g	6.44
Sodium mg	1669.42
Fibre g	3.04

Heat a large pan of lightly salted water to boiling point, then throw in the pasta. Cook it briskly according to the instructions on the pack until it is cooked but still *al dente*. Drain, add several tablespoons of sunflower oil and keep warm.

While the pasta is cooking put the leeks and chilli in a wide pan with the oil and cook very gently until the vegetables are soft without being burned. Add the well-rinsed and dried cockles to the leeks and heat through. Warm the brandy, pour it over the leeks and cockles and flame it, then add the cream.

At the same time put the wine in a large pan with the parsley and bring it to the boil. When it is boiling hard, throw in the mussels and cook for 2 - 3 minutes or until all their shells have opened; if any do not, discard them.

Add the mussels and their cooking liquid to the leeks and cockles. Season to taste.

To serve, pile the pasta in a large dish and spoon the fish mixture with its juices over the top. Serve at once.

Purchased sauces for pasta are a boon to a busy cook and there is no reason why being on a gluten- or wheat-free diet should change this. However, remember that they can be used not only with pasta but with potatoes, or even with rice, for a light supper dish.

Sunflower and Coriander Pesto

Serves 4

This makes an interesting change from the standard basil and pine nut pesto - and is very easy to make.

25 g	fresh coriander leaves	1 oz
50 g	sunflower seeds	2 oz
2	large cloves garlic, peeled	2
60 mL	olive oil	4 tbsp
	juice of 1 lemon	
	salt	
	pepper	

Put all the ingredients in the bowl of a small food processor and whizz until they are well chopped and amalgamated. Take care not to process them too much or they will become too solid. Toss the cooked hot pasta in the sauce and serve with fresh Parmesan and freshly ground black pepper.

PER SERVING	
Energy Kcals	212.23
Protein g	3.04
Fat g	21.13
Saturated fatty acids g	2.82
Monounsaturated fatty acids g	11.86
Polyunsaturated fatty acids g	5.71
Carbohydrate g	3.09
Total Sugars g	.59
Sodium mg	99.76
Fibre g	.87

Casseroles are always useful; in this day of the microwave you can leave it sitting in the fridge and merely heat up a slice as needed.

Curried Pasta Casserole

Serves 4

A "hearty" pasta dish for a cold evening.

250 g	wheat- and gluten-free pasta shapes	9 oz
25 g	butter	1 oz
2	small onions, peeled and finely chopped	2
1	large red pepper, seeded and finely chopped	1
30 mL	curry powder (check to make sure it is wheat- and gluten-free)	2 tbsp
200 g	spicy Italian sausage (check ingredients to make sure they do not include any wheat/gluten)	7 oz
400 g	tinned tomatoes	14 oz
	salt	
	pepper	
25 g	apricot jam (optional)	1 oz
150 mL	plain low-fat yogurt (gluten free)	5 fl oz

Cook the pasta according to the directions on the pack; drain thoroughly.

Meanwhile melt the butter in a pan and gently cook the onions and pepper with the curry powder until the vegetables are softening. Add the sausage, chopped up quite small, and the tomatoes with most of their juice. Cook them all together until the flavours are well amalgamated and everything heated well through. If the sauce is very runny, reduce it a bit by cooking it with the lid off the pan. Season to taste with salt and pepper and add the apricot jam.

Tip in the pasta and mix all well together and reheat, then turn into a serving dish and, just before serving, pour the yogurt over the top.

PER SERVING	
Energy Kcals	518.7
Protein g	16.4
Fat g	22.46
Saturated fatty acids g	5.11
Monounsaturated fatty acids g	3.31
Polyunsaturated fatty acids g	1.69
Carbohydrate g	67.07
Total Sugars g	17.86
Sodium mg	720.99
Fibre g	4.64

Basic Tomato Sauce

Serves 4

A useful basic tomato sauce for pasta - or indeed anything else!

450 g	onions, finely chopped	1 lb
3	large cloves garlic, finely chopped	3
1.5 kg	ripe tomatoes, roughly chopped	3 lb
5 mL	sugar	1 tsp
	salt	
	pepper	

Put the onions in a heavy pan with the garlic, tomatoes and sugar. Bring slowly to the boil and simmer gently for 30 - 45 minutes or until the juices are considerably reduced. Season with salt and pepper. Purée and sieve the sauce if you want it smooth. To vary the flavour of each serving, you can add a teaspoon of fresh or dried chopped herbs (almost any variety but basil is particularly Italian), half a chopped dried chilli, three finely chopped black olives or a couple of finely chopped anchovies - or anything else you fancy!

PER SERVING	
Energy Kcals	122.70
Protein g	4.34
Fat g	1.38
Saturated fatty acids g	1.50
Monounsaturated fatty acids g	1.54
Polyunsaturated fatty acids g	.87
Carbohydrate g	25.06
Total Sugars g	21.92
Sodium mg	134.70
Fibre g	5.48

For vegetarian children you could easily convert this into a "veggie" dish by substituting soya mince for the beef. However you will need to increase the liquid by about half as soya absorbs much more liquid than real meat.

Lasagne

Serves 6

A classic lasagne, this both freezes and reheats well.

60 mL	olive oil	4 tbsp
2	cloves garlic, chopped	2
2	medium onions, chopped	2
350 g	ground beef	12 oz
200 g	mushrooms, sliced	7 oz
350 g	ground beef	12 oz
30 mL	tomato purée	2 tbsp
2	tins (400 g) tomatoes	2
300 mL	red wine	10 fl oz
5 mL	dried thyme	1 tsp
100 g	wheat- and gluten-free pre-cooked lasagne sheets (see page 202)	4 oz
25 g	butter	1 oz
25 g	potato flour	1 oz
300 mL	milk	10 fl oz
150 mL	white wine	5 fl oz
60 mL	18% cream	4 tbsp
50 g	ricotta or other crumbly white cheese	2 oz
1	whole egg plus 1 egg yolk	1

Melt the oil in a large pan and gently fry the garlic and onion until they are beginning to soften. Turn up the heat, add the beef and fry it briskly for a couple of minutes. Reduce the heat again and add the mushrooms. Cook for about 5 minutes, then stir in the tomato purée, followed by the tomatoes, thyme and red wine. Bring to the boil and simmer gently, with the lid off, for 1 - 1 1/2 hours. Season to taste.

In an ovenproof dish layer the meat mixture with the pasta until both are used up, ideally starting and finishing with a meat layer.

Meanwhile, melt the butter in a pan, add the potato flour, cook for a few minutes, stirring continuously, then gradually add the milk, white wine and cream. Cook gently until the sauce thickens.

PER SERVING	
Energy Kcals	541.90
Protein g	22.38
Fat g	33.66
Saturated fatty acids g	14.40
Monounsaturated fatty acids g	17.49
Polyunsaturated fatty acids g	3.65
Carbohydrate g	27.19
Total Sugars g	10.35
Sodium mg	264.79
Fibre g	2.74

Pastas are effectively interchangeable, the only difference being in their shape. So always feel free to use another variety if your cupboard does not run to the one specified in the recipe.

Add the cheese and continue to cook until it is melted. Remove the pan from the heat, stir in the eggs and season to taste with salt and pepper. Pour the sauce over the lasagne and bake it in a medium oven (350°F / 180°C) for 30 minutes or until it is heated right through and the top is lightly browned. Serve at once.

Spaghetti with Smoked Salmon

Serves 4

This recipe can be quite economical if you use the smoked salmon offcuts which are now available in most supermarkets.

30 mL	olive oil	1 fl oz
100 g	button mushrooms, finely sliced	4 oz
250 mL	dry white wine	9 fl oz
15 mL, hpd	fresh dill, chopped or 1 tsp dried	1 hpd tsp
	small handful of fresh chives, chopped or 30 mL/ 2 heaped tsps dried	
300 mL	18% cream	10 fl oz
250 g	smoked salmon, cut in thin matchsticks	9 oz
	juice of 1 lemon	
250 g	gluten- and wheat-free spaghetti (see page 202 or use a commercial brand)	9 oz
	salt	
	pepper	

Heat the oil in a wide pan and gently fry the mushrooms for 4 - 5 minutes; do not let them colour. Add the wine, increase the heat and cook fast for a further 5 minutes to reduce the wine. Add the herbs and the cream, mix thoroughly, then add the salmon and reheat gently but do not boil or the sauce will curdle.

Season to taste with salt, pepper and lemon juice. Cover, set aside and keep just warm.

PER SERVING	
Energy Kcals	502.02
Protein g	28.87
Fat g	18.55
Saturated fatty acids g	5.75
Monounsaturated fatty acids g	8.97
Polyunsaturated fatty acids g	2.75
Carbohydrate g	48.54
Total Sugars g	4.24
Sodium mg	1331.5
Fibre g	2.13

Meanwhile cook the pasta according to the instructions on the pack until it is just *al dente*. Drain and rinse thoroughly with boiling water.

Turn the pasta into a warmed serving dish and gently mix in the salmon sauce before serving.

Although pasta is eaten throughout the country, Italian cooking varies enormously from the mountains in the north to the hot, flat, plains of southern Italy. This dish would find no favour in Naples!

Penne with Frankfurters and Spring Greens

Serves 4

Based on a northern Italian recipe, this is a hearty but flavoursome dish which goes down well with children - even though it does contain cabbage!

200 g	wheat- and gluten-free pasta, penne or macaroni (see page 202 or use a commercial brand)	7 oz
45 mL	olive oil	3 tbsp
200 g	onions, finely chopped	7 oz
400 g	spring greens, shredded	14 oz
200 mL	vegetable stock	7 fl oz
4	frankfurters (check to make sure they contain no starch or gluten), sliced into rounds	4
50 g	fresh Parmesan, grated	2 oz

PER SERVING	
Energy Kcals	602.04
Protein g	24.71
Fat g	34.73
Saturated fatty acids g	4.84
Monounsaturated fatty acids g	9.73
Polyunsaturated fatty acids g	2.42
Carbohydrate g	51.08
Total Sugars g	8.73
Sodium mg	8902.36
Fibre g	6.09

Cook the penne or macaroni according to the instructions on the pack until it is just *al dente*, then drain. Meanwhile, gently fry the onions in the oil until they start to soften but have not coloured. Add the spring greens and stock, cover and cook for 5 minutes or until the spring greens are starting to soften.

Slice the frankfurters into rounds, add to the spring greens and continue to cook for a further 5 minutes to allow the flavours to amalgamate. You should not need any further seasoning. Mix in the pasta, reheat then turn into a serving dish.

Grate the Parmesan over the dish and mix in well. Serve at once.

Right:
Pasta Primavera
(page 59)

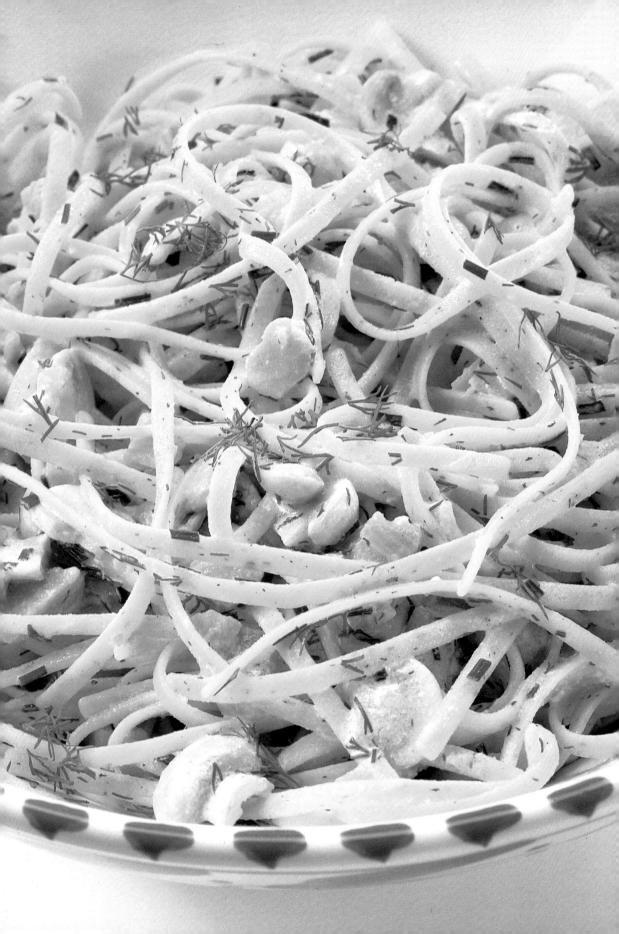

Certain tinned vegetables (artichokes, pulses such as chick peas, corn, waterchestnuts and olives are my favourites) are invaluable to have in your store cupboard. No matter how little else you may have, combined with rice or even on their own they make an excellent and quick meal.

Pasta Primavera

Serves 4

A quick and easy pasta dish. To make it vegetarian or vegan, leave out the ham and replace the cream with soya cream.

450 g	wheat- and gluten-free pasta shapes of your choice (see page 202 or use a commercial brand)	1 lb
45 mL	sunflower oil	3 tbsp
2	medium leeks, finely sliced	2
4	sticks celery, finely chopped	4
100 g	mushrooms, finely sliced	4 oz
200 g	tinned artichokes, drained and quartered	7 oz
50 g	chopped ham	2 oz
150 mL	18% cream	5 fl oz
300 mL	dry white wine	10 fl oz
	juice of 1 lemon	
	salt	
	pepper	
	a handful of fresh parsley, chopped	

Heat the oil in a heavy pan and gently cook the leek and celery until soft; add the mushrooms and continue to cook for a few minutes. Add the artichokes and the ham, then the cream and the wine. Mix well and allow to simmer for a few minutes. Add the lemon juice and season to taste. Set aside to keep warm.

Cook the pasta in plenty of fast boiling water according to the instructions on the pack until it is just cooked or *al dente*. Drain the noodles quickly and turn them into a dish. Stir the parsley into the sauce, spoon it over the noodles and serve at once.

PER SERVING	
Energy Kcals	666.31
Protein g	19.97
Fat g	23.52
Saturated fatty acids g	8.30
Monounsaturated fatty acids g	7.56
Polyunsaturated fatty acids g	9.36
Carbohydrate g	88.11
Total Sugars g	7.82
Sodium mg	286.81
Fibre g	5.38

Left:
Pizza Base and Tomato Sauce (page 136)

Avocados are always difficult to judge and so disappointing if they are rock hard. I find it best to go for the Hass variety which get darker as they ripen so you do know that when they are black they are ready to eat.

Avocado and Bacon Salad

Serves 4

A more elegant version of the ever popular avocado and bacon sandwich - excellent for lunch or a substantial starter.

150 g	gluten/wheat-free pasta shells (see page 202 or use a commercial brand)	5 oz
30 mL	olive oil	2 tbsp
2	medium leeks, peeled and finely sliced	2
6	slices of lean back bacon	6
1	large ripe avocado	1
50 g	pine nuts, lightly crushed	2 oz
	about 20 leaves of fresh basil	
	juice of 1 large lemon	
	salt	
	freshly ground black pepper	

Heat the oil in a heavy pan and gently cook the leeks for 10 - 15 minutes until they are quite soft.

Cook the bacon briskly until it is brown and crisp on both sides. "Dry" it off on some paper towel to remove any excess grease and chop it into small pieces.

Meanwhile, cook the pasta in plenty of lightly salted boiling water until it is *al dente*. How long this will take will depend on the type of pasta (rice or corn based) that you are using. Drain it and tip it into a serving bowl. Dribble over some of the olive oil and mix well.

Carefully core, peel and dice the avocado.

Mix the leeks, bacon and avocado with the pasta, stirring it gently to avoid damaging the avocado pieces.

Add the pine nuts, chopped basil leaves, lemon juice and salt and pepper to taste.

Serve at once as a starter or light luncheon salad.

PER SERVING	
Energy Kcals	609.48
Protein g	17.02
Fat g	48.87
Saturated fatty acids g	12.97
Monounsaturated fatty acids g	23.76
Polyunsaturated fatty acids g	10.19
Carbohydrate g	27.73
Total Sugars g	3.42
Sodium mg	1128.68
Fibre g	5.70

It is a good idea to make two or three times the amount of sauce that you need and freeze the extra in small containers, ready for use at a moment's notice.

Spaghetti Bolognese

Serves 6

The addition of chicken livers not only adds a depth of flavour to this recipe but increases one's intake of Vitamin A.

15 mL	olive oil	1 tbsp
75 g	lean bacon slices	3 oz
1	medium onion, finely chopped	1
1	medium carrot, finely chopped	1
1	small stick celery, finely chopped	1
250 g	lean ground beef	9 oz
100 g	chopped chicken livers	4 oz
30 mL	tomato purée	2 tbsp
100 mL	dry white wine	4 fl oz
200 mL	water or vegetable stock	7 fl oz
	salt, pepper and nutmeg	
300 g	wheat- and gluten-free spaghetti (see page 202 or use a commercial brand)	10 oz

Heat the oil in a heavy, deep pan and gently brown the bacon. Add the onion, carrot and celery and continue to cook until they are brown. Add the beef and turn regularly so that it browns easily. Add the chicken livers, then, in a couple of minutes, the tomato purée and white wine. Season lightly with the salt, pepper and a pinch of nutmeg and add the stock or water, cover the pan and simmer very gently for 30 - 40 minutes.

Meanwhile cook the spaghetti according to the instructions on the pack.

To serve mix the sauce well into the pasta and serve at once. Serve grated Parmesan cheese with it if you like.

PER SERVING	
Energy Kcals	412.43
Protein g	19.46
Fat g	18.73
Saturated fatty acids g	5.94
Monounsaturated fatty acids g	8.02
Polyunsaturated fatty acids g	1.43
Carbohydrate g	41.72
Total Sugars g	4.29
Sodium mg	332.46
Fibre g	2.41

If you wanted to make this dish more "adult" you could add a handful of whole blanched almonds to the sauce before mixing in the pasta and broccoli.

Pasta and Broccoli au Gratin

Serves 4

A more filling version of a classic broccoli with cheese sauce. Very popular with children!

150 g	wheat- and gluten-free pasta shapes (see page 202 or use a commercial brand)	5 oz
300 g	broccoli florets	10 oz
1	medium onion, chopped very roughly	1
25 g	butter	1 oz
25 g	potato flour	1 oz
300 mL	milk	10 fl oz
100 mL	dry white wine	4 fl oz
200 g	strong cheddar cheese, grated	7 oz
25 g	whole-grain mustard (check that it is wheat- and gluten-free)	1 oz
	salt	
	pepper	

Cook the pasta according to the instructions on the package, drain and keep warm.

Cook the broccoli and onion in a steamer until they are just cooked but still slightly *al dente*. Save the water from steaming.

Meanwhile, heat the butter in a pan and add the potato flour. Slowly add the milk and wine and continue to heat, stirring continuously, until the sauce thickens. Add three quarters of the cheese and the mustard, then season to taste. If the sauce is a bit thick, thin it with a few spoonfuls of the water from the broccoli.

Gently mix the pasta into the broccoli and onion, then spoon both into a warmed casserole or pie dish. Spoon over the sauce and sprinkle the remaining cheese over the top and brown under the broiler. Serve at once.

PER SERVING	
Energy Kcals	511.56
Protein g	24.40
Fat g	27.33
Saturated fatty acids g	16.59
Monounsaturated fatty acids g	7.64
Polyunsaturated fatty acids g	1.79
Carbohydrate g	40.60
Total Sugars g	7.62
Sodium mg	586.81
Fibre g	4.13

Do not be tempted to buy mini vegetables instead of young ones. They may look pretty but they have very little flavour.

Pasta Rusticano

Serves 4

A good pasta dish when there are vegetarians around. You can successfully serve it to both meat eaters and veggies!

200 g	gluten-free pasta - brown rice macaroni works very well in this dish - (see page 202 or use a commercial brand)	7 oz
2	young carrots, sliced in thin rounds	2
2	sticks celery, diced	2
1	medium onion, peeled and chopped roughly	1
1	large zucchini, sliced in rounds	1
2	cloves garlic, sliced thinly	2
5 mL	dried marjoram	1 tsp
10 mL	dried oregano	2 tsp
400 g	tinned tomatoes	14 oz
100 mL	dry white wine	4 oz
200 g	tinned or frozen broad beans - or fresh young broad beans, cooked for 5 minutes in lightly salted water	7 oz
	salt	
	pepper	
75 g	freshly grated Parmesan	3 oz

Put the carrots, celery, onion, zucchini, garlic and herbs in a heavy pan with the tomatoes and the white wine.

Bring to the boil, cover and simmer for 10 - 15 minutes or until the carrots and celery are just cooked but still slightly crunchy. Add the broad beans and season to taste with salt and pepper. Continue to cook for another few minutes to warm the beans through.

Meanwhile, boil the macaroni in plenty of lightly salted water until just *al dente,* then drain and keep warm.

Carefully fold the pasta into the vegetables and serve at once, heavily sprinkled with Parmesan.

PER SERVING	
Energy Kcals	353.97
Protein g	15.10
Fat g	7.19
Saturated fatty acids g	5.45
Monounsaturated fatty acids g	3.86
Polyunsaturated fatty acids g	1.61
Carbohydrate g	52.55
Total Sugars g	7.28
Sodium mg	471.86
Fibre g	5.30

You could make this in individual bowls to be stored in the refrigerator so that children could heat it up for themselves when they are hungry.

Tuna and Corn Macaroni

Serves 4

Another great success with children as it combines three of their favourite foods - pasta, corn and tuna - although you may need to leave the parsley out for some!

200 g	gluten- and wheat-free macaroni (see page 202 or use a commercial brand)	7 oz
60 mL	sunflower oil	4 tbsp
150 g	button mushrooms, sliced	5 oz
25 g	potato flour	1 oz
500 mL	milk	18 fl oz
200 g	tinned corn niblets, drained	7 oz
200 g	tinned tuna, drained and flaked	7 oz
	juice of 1 large lemon	
	salt	
	pepper	
2	large handfuls of parsley, chopped	2

Cook the pasta according to the instructions on the package until just *al dente* - drain and keep warm.

Heat the oil in a heavy pan and gently cook the mushrooms for 5 minutes. Add the potato flour, stir well, then gradually add the milk. Bring back to the simmer and cook until the sauce thickens. Add the corn and the tuna and mix well. Season to taste with the lemon juice, salt and pepper, then mix in the pasta. If necessary, thin the sauce with a little extra milk. Just before serving stir in the parsley.

PER SERVING	
Energy Kcals	560.03
Protein g	28.22
Fat g	27.33
Saturated fatty acids g	6.05
Monounsaturated fatty acids g	6.59
Polyunsaturated fatty acids g	13.16
Carbohydrate g	54.35
Total Sugars g	9.77
Sodium mg	488.96
Fibre g	6.71

Since I have never yet come across a gluten- and wheat-free ravioli this is something that you really may have to make for yourself. However, take heart as it really is not very difficult. If you are nervous make sure that you have plenty of sauce to pour over the top. Even if the ravioli fall to pieces they will taste good and no one will see if they are covered with sauce!

Frankfurter and Cheese Ravioli

Serves 6

Surprisingly easy to make, these ravioli are really tasty. If you find them a little dry on their own or just with oil you could serve them with the tomato sauce on page 55.

370 g	fresh gram pasta (see page 50) made into lasagne sheets	13 oz
4	frankfurters (check ingredients to ensure they do not include wheat or gluten)	4
75 g	Cheddar cheese, cut into very thin slivers	3 oz
60 mL	olive oil	4 tbsp
50 g	freshly grated Parmesan	2 oz

Lay out the freshly made lasagne sheets on a floured board. Halve them, then cut both halves into 12 large or 18 smaller squares.

Cut the frankfurters into 3 cm (1 inch) lengths, then cut them in half down their length. Lay out the frankfurters on the squares of pasta and cover them with the slivers of cheese. Brush the edges of the ravioli with water, then cover them with the other square of pasta. Press the edges down firmLy. Place the ravioli on a plate, cover with damp paper towel and leave in the fridge for at least half an hour.

Heat a large pan of lightly salted water. When it is boiling gently lift the ravioli in with a slotted spoon. Simmer them gently for 4 - 5 minutes or until the pasta is cooked. Remove to a heated serving dish, dribble with the olive oil, sprinkle with the Parmesan and some freshly ground black pepper and serve at once.

PER SERVING	
Energy Kcals	407.23
Protein g	18.39
Fat g	26.88
Saturated fatty acids g	6.61
Monounsaturated fatty acids g	10.24
Polyunsaturated fatty acids g	2.51
Carbohydrate g	24.20
Total Sugars g	1.40
Sodium mg	444.77
Fibre g	3.76

Vegan Pasta with Spinach and Broad Beans

Serves 6

This sauce will be good for vegetarian teenagers - as well as being simple, quick and easy.

15 mL	cornstarch	1 tbsp
15 mL	tomato purée	1 tbsp
200 mL	tomato juice	7 fl oz
225 g	frozen leaf spinach, drained	8 oz
200 g	can of broad beans	7 oz
225 g	firm tofu, cut into small dice (you can use a smoked tofu if you prefer a smoky flavour - but check the ingredients on the pack)	8 oz
	salt, pepper and nutmeg to taste	
350 g	gluten- and wheat-free pasta of your choice	12 oz

Mix the cornstarch with the tomato purée, then add the tomato juice to make a smooth purée. Heat slowly, stirring continually, till the sauce thickens. Add the spinach, broad beans and tofu, mix well, then season to taste with the salt, pepper and nutmeg.

Cook the pasta in plenty of fast boiling water according to the instructions on the package. Reheat the sauce gently and serve spooned over the pasta.

PER SERVING	
Energy Kcals	322.00
Protein g	10.10
Fat g	6.03
Saturated fatty acids g	0.80
Monounsaturated fatty acids g	3.25
Polyunsaturated fatty acids g	1.98
Carbohydrate g	56.70
Total Sugars g	8.15
Sodium mg	453.00
Fibre g	4.80

Poultry, Meat and Game

Coq au Vin Blanc

Turkey with Artichoke Hearts
and Orange Sauce

Chicken Satay

Chicken Breasts Braised with
Noodles and Mushrooms

Chicken Kiev

Chicken Nuggets

Lemon Chicken in Batter with Lemon
Sauce

Chicken Breasts with Coconut Milk

Chicken Breasts Stuffed
with Smoked Salmon

Chicken Rosti

Chicken and Asparagus Casserole

Chicken with Okra, Chilli and
Bananas

Chicken Risotto with Fennel and Pine
Nuts

Chilli Pancakes

"Battered" Meat Loaf

Paprika Beef with Brandy and Cream

Corn and Beef Hash Casserole

Beef Crumble

Filet de Boeuf a L'Italienne

Steak and Kidney Pie

Cassoulet

Spring Lamb en Croute

Lamb Casserole

Rack of Lamb with Mustard Crust

Curried Lamb with Greek Yogurt

Bobotie

Leg of Lamb Casserole with Beans
and Green Peppercorns

Leg of Lamb with Zucchini and
Lima Beans

Alternative Moussaka

Pork Sausages

Pork Sausages with Polenta

Ham and Chicory Stuffed Pancakes

Sweet and Sour Pork

Pork Fillet with Artichokes
and Orange

Cauliflower Cheese with Bacon and
Green Peas

Pheasant Braised with White Grapes

Duck with Apple and Orange Sauce

Risotto of Squab and Wild Rice

If you cannot get button onions you could use pickling onions, although they are very fiddly to peel. If neither are available use 1 large Spanish onion, chopped roughly.

Coq au Vin Blanc

Serves 6

In this white version of the classic French dish, the white wine gives a slightly lighter texture to the sauce without losing any of its flavour.

15 mL	butter	1 tbsp
30 mL	olive oil	2 tbsp
100 g	unsalted bacon, diced	4 oz
20	button onions	20
2	cloves garlic, finely chopped	2
225 g	button mushrooms, wiped	8 oz
6	chicken joints, breast or legs as you prefer	6
25 g	lightly seasoned potato flour	1 oz
2	bouquet garni	2
90 mL	water	6 tbsp
20	baby new potatoes	20
45 mL	brandy	3 tbsp
200 mL	full bodied, but not sweet, white wine - Muscadet is quite good	7 fl oz
15 g	soft butter	½ oz
15 g	potato flour	½ oz
	large handful of fresh parsley, chopped	

Heat the oven to 180°C / 350°F.

Melt the butter and oil in a heavy casserole and briskly fry the bacon, onions and garlic until they are beginning to soften. Add the mushrooms and continue to cook until the vegetables are all golden but not burnt. Remove them with a slotted spoon and keep them warm. Toss the chicken joints in the seasoned flour and sauté them in the butter and oil until they too are golden on both sides.

Return the vegetables to the casserole, add the bouquet garni and the water, cover the casserole and cook it in the oven for 30 - 40 minutes or until the chicken is really tender.

Meanwhile, steam or boil the potatoes until cooked, drain them and keep them warm.

When they are done, remove the chicken and vegetables from

the pot, arrange them in a serving dish with the potatoes and keep them warm.

Skim as much extra fat off the juices as possible. Warm the brandy in a ladle, pour it onto the juices and light it. Let it burn for a minute or two, then pour on the wine and water. Stir thoroughly to make sure you get any burned bits off the bottom of the pan, then cook briskly for 5 - 10 minutes to reduce the quantity slightly.

Mix the softened butter with the potato flour and add it, in small pieces, to the sauce. Continue to cook it until it thickens. Adjust the seasoning to taste, then pour the sauce over the chicken and vegetables.

Sprinkle liberally with the chopped parsley and serve at once.

Turkey with Artichoke Hearts and Orange Sauce

Serves 6

Now that it is easy to buy turkey pieces rather than the whole bird it can be eaten every day, not just at Christmas. If you do not like the slightly stronger taste of the turkey you can use the recipe with chicken breasts.

700 g	boneless turkey fillets	1 lb 9oz
30 mL	olive oil	2 tbsp
2	onions , very finely sliced	2
200 g	celery , chopped small	7 oz
15 g	potato flour	1/2 oz
225 g	artichoke hearts, freshly cooked, frozen or tinned and drained	8 oz
	rind and juice of 4 oranges	
	salt	
	pepper	

Put the turkey pieces with an extra onion and carrot and approximately 600 mL/1 pint of water in a pan and bring them slowly to the boil. Simmer them gently for 25 - 30 minutes or until the meat is just cooked, then remove the turkey and strain and reserve the stock.

PER SERVING	
Energy Kcals	450.15
Protein g	36.57
Fat g	20.92
Saturated fatty acids g	7.30
Monounsaturated fatty acids g	11.31
Polyunsaturated fatty acids g	2.84
Carbohydrate g	20.91
Total Sugars g	3.75
Sodium mg	401.47
Fibre g	2.34

If you buy your turkey on the bone rather than off you can make an excellent stock from the bones with a few vegetables. If you add a little rice or a few lentils to the stock, simmer it for half an hour and season it to taste, you will have an instant and cost-free soup.

PER SERVING	
Energy Kcals	214.15
Protein g	28.83
Fat g	7.15
Saturated fatty acids g	2.81
Monounsaturated fatty acids g	5.84
Polyunsaturated fatty acids g	1.92
Carbohydrate g	11
Total Sugars g	8.09
Sodium mg	205.27
Fibre g	1.10

Meanwhile, heat the oil in a pan and slowly cook the onions and celery until they are soft but not coloured. Add the potato flour then, gradually, 450 mL/15 fl oz of the reserved stock, the rind and juice of two of the oranges and the artichoke hearts. Cook all together for a couple of minutes until the sauce has thickened, then add the turkey pieces, heat the dish through thoroughly and season to taste with salt and pepper.

Transfer it into a warmed serving dish and decorate with the remaining two oranges, neatly segmented, before serving with rice or new potatoes and a green vegetable.

Because of the publicity given to peanut allergy these days many people are avoiding peanuts altogether. However, as long as you do not have an allergy to them they are extremely nutritious, not to mention delicious. Very useful for a wheat- or gluten-allergic person to carry with them in case they feel hungry when nothing else wheat- and gluten-free is available.

Chicken Satay

Serves 6

This popular eastern dish can be served either as a main course with rice or on little sticks as a cocktail or buffet dish. In the latter case, hand a dish of the sauce out with the satay sticks - plus some napkins!

6	chicken breasts, bone removed	6
25 g	ground almonds	1 oz
15 mL	shredded root ginger	1 tbsp
5 mL	ground coriander	1 tsp
5 mL	ground turmeric	1 tsp
5 mL	dark brown sugar	1 tsp
300 mL	coconut milk	10 fl oz
30 mL	sunflower oil	2 tbsp
2.5 mL	chilli powder	1/2 tsp
250 g	onions, very finely chopped	9 oz
225 g	peanut butter (check ingredients list for wheat or gluten)	8 oz
5 mL	light brown sugar	1 tsp
15 mL	gluten-free soya sauce	1 tbsp
	juice of 1/2 a lemon or lime	

Heat the oven to 180°C / 350°F .

Mix the almonds, ginger, spices and sugar. Add the coconut milk, mix well, then use this to marinade the chicken breasts for about 2 hours. Transfer the breasts, with the marinade, to an ovenproof dish, cover them and bake for 40 minutes. Meanwhile, heat the oil in a pan with the chilli powder and sweat the onions until they are quite soft. Take off the heat and add the peanut butter and all the other ingredients to taste.

Meanwhile, cook plenty of brown or white rice to accompany the satay.

When the chicken is done, remove it from the oven, add the cooking juices to the sauce mixture, adjust the seasoning to taste and spoon over the chicken before serving with a good green salad and lots of rice. If serving as a cocktail snack, cut chicken into bite-size pieces and thread on to bamboo sticks.

PER SERVING	
Energy Kcals	733.35
Protein g	49.26
Fat g	55.25
Saturated fatty acids g	12.54
Monounsaturated fatty acids g	25.35
Polyunsaturated fatty acids g	15.76
Carbohydrate g	10.93
Total Sugars g	8.46
Sodium mg	338.44
Fibre g	3.65

Chicken Breasts Braised with Noodles and Mushrooms

Serves 4

This dish can be made with chicken breast or legs, depending on whether you prefer dark or light meat. Even though it is a bore, it is worth skinning the tomatoes.

60 mL	olive oil	4 tbsp
50 g	leeks, trimmed and sliced thinly	2 oz
200 g	zucchini, topped, tailed and sliced thickly	7 oz
150 g	tomatoes, peeled (dunk in boiling water for 1 minute then peel off skin) and chopped	5 oz
4	chicken breasts, skin removed	4
100 g	field mushrooms, thickly sliced	4 oz
200 g	gluten- and wheat-free noodles (see page 202 or use a commercial brand)	7 oz
	sea salt	
	freshly ground black pepper	

Heat 30 mL / 2 tablespoons of the oil in a heavy pan and add the leeks.

PER SERVING	
Energy Kcals	411.85
Protein g	17.25
Fat g	18.23
Saturated fatty acids g	3.10
Polyunsaturated fatty acids g	2.47
Monounsaturated fatty acids g	12.49
Carbohydrate g	43.28
Total Sugars g	2.34
Fibre g	1.38
Sodium mg	256.51

A real party dish which few people are prepared to tackle at home although it is not that difficult as long as you do not try to rush the chilling of each operation.

Cook briskly for a couple of minutes, then add the sliced zucchini. Continue to cook for another few minutes then add the tomatoes. Turn the heat down, place the chicken portions on top of the vegetables and cover the pan. Simmer gently for 30 minutes or until the chicken is cooked, then adjust the seasoning to taste.

Meanwhile, heat the remaining oil in a small pan and cook the mushrooms lightly.

Cook the noodles briskly in plenty of fast boiling water for 3 - 4 minutes, drain briefly, then mix with the mushrooms.

Serve the chicken with its vegetables accompanied by the mushrooms and noodles.

Chicken Kiev

Serves 4

The secret to keeping the butter inside the chicken breast is to chill the breast well between every stage of preparation.

100 g	butter	4 oz
4	cloves garlic, crushed	4
	large handful of fresh parsley, chopped fine	
	good squeeze of fresh lemon juice	
4	chicken breasts	4
100 g	cornflakes (gluten free), crushed	4 oz
30 g	potato flour	1 1/2 oz
2	large eggs, beaten	2

Soften the butter thoroughly, add the garlic, parsley and a squeeze of lemon juice and beat well. Divide into 4 portions, shape into rectangles and put in the freezer for at least an hour.

With a sharp knife split the breasts in half horizontally but do not cut all the way through. Open them out flat on wet greaseproof paper. Cover with more wet greaseproof paper, then beat them flat with a rolling pin.

Put the cornflakes in a plastic bag and crush them thoroughly with a rolling pin - they should be almost powdered - then mix with the potato flour.

Place one piece of butter inside each breast then roll the breast so that the butter is sealed inside. Roll each breast in the egg and then in the cornflake mixture. Chill in the refrigerator for 30 minutes.

PER SERVING	
Energy Kcals	501.49
Protein g	32.75
Fat g	29.43
Saturated fatty acids g	16.26
Monounsaturated fatty acids g	8.8
Polyunsaturated fatty acids g	2.18
Carbohydrate g	28.74
Total Sugars g	3.08
Sodium mg	612.88
Fibre g	1.17

Take out and roll again in the egg and cornflakes then return to the refrigerator for another 30 minutes.

Meanwhile heat the oven to 180°C / 350°F.

Place the chicken breasts on a rack over a baking tray and bake in the oven for 20 - 30 minutes or until the crust is crisp and tanned and the breasts are cooked.

Remove carefully onto a heated serving dish and serve at once with a selection of green vegetables.

Although intended for children these nuggets can also be used as a cocktail snack with a dipping sauce.

Chicken Nuggets

Serves 6

You can substitute plain gluten-free potato chips for the cornflakes for these nuggets or use the batter on the recipe for Lemon Chicken on page 74.

600 g	lean chicken meat, cubed or diced into whatever size nuggets you need	1 lb 5oz
2	eggs, beaten	2
200 g	cornflakes (gluten free)	7 oz
50 g	potato flour	2 oz
	vegetable oil for deep frying	

Crush the cornflakes as small as you can by putting them into a plastic bag then rolling them with a rolling pin. Turn them into a flattish dish and add the potato flour - mix well.

Roll the chicken cubes in the beaten egg.

Roll the well-egged nuggets in the cornflake mixture until they are completely coated. Set them aside in a covered dish, in the fridge, for an hour or so.

Heat the oil in a deep pan or a deep fryer until a piece of stale bread turns brown in 1 minute.

Deep fry the nuggets for approximately 7 minutes or until the coating is crisp and lightly browned and the middle is cooked but not dried up. Drain on paper towels and serve at once.

PER SERVING	
Energy Kcals	432.58
Protein g	26.54
Fat g	21.75
Saturated fatty acids g	3.63
Monounsaturated fatty acids g	8.18
Polyunsaturated fatty acids g	8.41
Carbohydrate g	35.13
Total Sugars g	3.15
Sodium mg	481.73
Fibre g	.78

Do not use ordinary bread cubes when testing the heat of the oil as they could contaminate the oil with a tiny amount of gluten.

Lemon Chicken in Batter with Lemon Sauce

Serves 4

The lemon in this recipe gives it a real tang. You can make all the bits in advance so that you only have to deep fry the chicken breasts before you serve them.

4	chicken breasts	4
15	coriander seeds, lightly crushed	15
	small pinch salt	
2	grinds black pepper	2
	grated rind and juice of 2 lemons	
100 g	sifted chick pea (gram) flour	4 oz
450 mL	water	16 fl oz
	small pinch salt	
25 g	butter	1 oz
5 mL, hpd	potato flour	1 hpd tsp
	vegetable oil for deep frying	

Marinade

Lay out the chicken breasts in a flat dish. Cover them with the crushed coriander seeds and a light sprinkling of salt and pepper. Pour over the juice of the 2 lemons. Cover and leave for at least 1 hour.

Batter

Make the batter by mixing the sifted gram flour, a small pinch of salt, the lemon rind and 200 mL of the water in a food processor.

Lemon sauce

Remove the chicken breasts and set aside. Strain the marinade into a small saucepan, add the butter and melt slowly. Add the potato flour, stir well, then gradually add the remaining water. Bring to the boil and cook gently until the sauce thickens. Keep warm.

To serve

Heat the oil in a large pan or deep fryer until a small piece of stale gluten- and wheat-free bread turns brown in 1 minute.

Dip the chicken breasts in the batter and make sure they are well covered. Gently lower each breast into the oil and cook fairly gently for 5 minutes. Increase the heat under the oil and continue to cook the breasts until their batter is crisp and browned. Remove

PER SERVING	
Energy Kcals	270.91
Protein g	30.90
Fat g	11.34
Saturated fatty acids g	4.89
Monounsaturated fatty acids g	3.99
Polyunsaturated fatty acids g	2.15
Carbohydrate g	13.50
Total Sugars g	1.20
Sodium mg	246.65
Fibre g	2.75

and drain briefly on paper towel. Serve at once with the lemon sauce.

Chicken Breasts with Coconut Milk

Serves 6

A delicious low-calorie, low-fat chicken dish with a strong hint of the Far East.

30 mL	olive oil	2 tbsp
200 g	leeks, trimmed and very finely sliced	7 oz
200 g	fennel, trimmed and very finely sliced	7 oz
6	cooked chicken breasts	6
200 g	fresh spinach, chopped (or frozen leaf spinach, defrosted)	7 oz
800 mL	coconut milk	1½ pints
25 g	potato flour	1 oz
	a handful of fresh coriander leaves, chopped	
	juice of 1 - 2 fresh limes	
	salt	
	white pepper	

Heat the oil in a wide, heavy pan, add the leeks and fennel, cover and sweat gently for 15 - 20 minutes or until the vegetables are quite soft. Add the chicken breasts with the spinach. Mix the potato flour with a little of the coconut milk to make a smooth paste, then add that, along with the rest of the coconut milk. Cover the pan again and continue to cook gently until the chicken breasts are cooked through and the sauce has thickened slightly. Add the coriander, chopped, the lime juice and salt and pepper to taste. Serve at once with plenty of basmati rice and a salad or a green vegetable such as snow peas.

If fresh coriander is difficult to get, you can always substitute fresh parsley. The flavour will be different but still good. This would be better than using dried coriander leaf which really needs long cooking to bring out its flavour.

PER SERVING	
Energy Kcals	210.57
Protein g	22.5
Fat g	8.09
Saturated fatty acids g	2.1
Monounsaturated fatty acids g	6.52
Polyunsaturated fatty acids g	2.92
Carbohydrate g	12.92
Total Sugars g	8.79
Sodium mg	373.32
Fibre g	3.58

Chicken Breasts Stuffed with Smoked Salmon

Serves 4

These chicken breasts are also good cold in which case leave them to get quite cold before removing them from the parcels. Slice with a very sharp knife and serve with a salad. The salmon can be quite cheap if you buy off cuts.

60 mL	olive oil	4 tbsp
250 g	leeks, trimmed	9 oz
5	cloves of garlic, peeled and thinly sliced	5
150 g	white glutinous rice or risotto rice	5 oz
25 g	sun-dried tomatoes, chopped	1 oz
500 g	celeriac, peeled and diced	1 lb 2oz
950 mL	water or unsalted vegetable stock	1¾ pints
100 g	smoked salmon pieces	3½ oz
4	chicken breasts	4

Warm half the oil in a heavy pan and add half the leeks and 3 of the garlic cloves. Cook gently for about 5 minutes or until they are just softened. Add the rice, stir around for a few minutes, then add the stock. Bring to the boil and simmer briskly for 15 - 20 minutes or until the water is absorbed and the rice is soft.

Meanwhile, put the rest of the oil into a deep casserole dish with the rest of the leeks and garlic, the tomatoes, celeriac and 45 to 60 mL / 3 or 4 tablespoons of the water or stock. Bring to the boil and simmer for 5 - 10 minutes.

Put 60 mL / 4 tablespoons of the rice mixture into a bowl and mix in the smoked salmon pieces.

Lay two of the chicken breasts out on a flat surface, cover them with wet greaseproof paper and beat them flat with a mallet. Remove the greaseproof paper and cover the breasts with half the rice each. Top them with the other chicken breasts. Lay out 2 new J cloths or muslin cloths and place one of the chicken breast parcels on each. Fold the corners up to make a loose parcel so that the stuffing does not fall out in the cooking.

Carefully lift the two parcels and put them on top of the simmering celeriac. Cover the casserole and simmer for 35 - 45 minutes or until the chicken is quite cooked and the celeriac soft.

Carefully remove the two parcels from the pot, leave them to rest

PER SERVING	
Energy Kcals	465.63
Protein g	34.58
Fat g	20.83
Saturated fatty acids g	3.35
Monounsaturated fatty acids g	11.93
Polyunsaturated fatty acids g	3.89
Carbohydrate g	34.06
Total Sugars g	3.87
Sodium mg	708.5
Fibre g	6.26

You can also use the potatoes on their own as a vegetable to go with a roast of meat - or just as a crunchy supper dish.

for about half an hour, then untie them. Gently reheat the remaining rice. With a very sharp knife slice the chicken breasts thickly across into 4 - 6 slices. Lift carefully onto the serving dish or plates and serve with a spoonful of the remaining rice and the celeriac with its juices.

You could also serve a green vegetable such a broccoli or a green salad.

Chicken Rosti

Serves 4

An unusual version of a favourite Swiss dish.

4	boned chicken breasts	4
100 g	Gruyère cheese, sliced	3½ oz
500 g	baking potatoes, scrubbed	1 lb 2 oz
200 g	onions	7 oz

Heat the oven to 350°F/ 180°C.

Open up the chicken breasts horizontally, like a book. Divide the cheese into four and lay ¼ inside each breast. Fold over the breast to make a square parcel and set aside.

Grate the scrubbed potatoes coarsely (you can leave their skins on) and slice the onion thinly. Mix the two together. Place the four breasts in the bottom of a large baking dish (ideally one from which you can serve) and spread the potato and onion mixture over them. Cover lightly with a piece of foil and bake for 20 minutes. Remove from the oven, remove the foil and mix the potatoes around slightly if their edges look as though they are getting burned, then return to the oven for a further 20 minutes to crisp the top of the potatoes.

Serve at once with a green vegetable or salad.

PER SERVING	
Energy Kcals	444.00
Protein g	27.63
Fat g	26.38
Saturated fatty acids g	12.85
Polyunsaturated fatty acids g	3.73
Monounsaturated fatty acids g	11.68
Carbohydrate g	25.70
Total Sugars g	3.80
Fibre g	2.33
Sodium mg	247.75

Chicken and Asparagus Casserole

Serves 6

This is an excellent casserole for a cold summer lunch or supper although it also tastes good hot. If you wish to economize you could use asparagus pieces rather than tips.

1.5 kg	whole chicken	3 lb 5 oz
50 g	cornstarch	2 oz
100 mL	home-made chicken stock / water	4 fl oz
100 mL	dry white wine	4 fl oz
100 mL	whole milk	4 fl oz
100 mL	whipping cream	4 fl oz
1	tin (400 g) of asparagus spears, drained	1
75 g	rice flour	3 oz
150 g	chick pea / gram flour	5 oz
100 g	low-fat spread	4 oz
75 mL	water	5 tbsp
	sea salt	
	black pepper	

Roast the chicken in a moderate oven for 45 - 60 minutes or until it is quite cooked. Remove from the oven, cool slightly, then remove the flesh from the bones, tear it into smallish pieces and set aside. Put the bones in a large saucepan with a couple of chopped onions and carrots and 2 - 3 L / 3 - 4 pints of water. Bring to the boil and simmer for 1 - 1 ½ hours, then drain off the stock and set aside 100 mL / 3 ½ fl oz of it. The rest can be used for soup.

Meanwhile, rub the fat into the mixed rice and gram flour. Add approximately 75 mL / 5 tablespoons of water to make a soft (but not sticky) dough. Cover and leave it to rest in the fridge.

Mix the cornstarch with a little of the 100 mL / 4 fl oz of stock to make a smooth paste, then add the rest of the stock, the white wine and the milk. Gradually bring to the boil over a slow heat, stirring constantly to prevent it going lumpy.

Open the asparagus and drain off the liquid. Add this to the sauce along with the chicken pieces and the cream. Bring back to the boil and season to taste with salt and pepper. Finally add the asparagus tips taking care to mix them in gently so they do not get broken.

PER SERVING	
Energy Kcals	491.83
Protein g	32.92
Fat g	24.11
Saturated fatty acids g	8.87
Monounsaturated fatty acids g	7.58
Polyunsaturated fatty acids g	3.53
Carbohydrate g	34.16
Total Sugars g	3.17
Sodium mg	3195.79
Fibre g	4.87

Half a banana, mashed or finely chopped, makes an excellent addition to many meat casserole dishes as it gives them a richness of taste and texture without actually making them taste of banana.

Spoon the mixture into a pie dish.

Roll the pastry out carefully until it is quite a bit larger than the pie dish. It should be quite thick to hold together.

Place the pie dish on the paste and cut out a pie dish shape. Then cut out a border the width of the pie dish rim from the scraps. Wet the rim of the pie dish and line it with the cut-out scraps. Wet the top of the pastry border then carefully, using a spatula and a rolling pin, lift the pastry top onto the top of the pie. Press the edges down with your thumbs and use the scraps to decorate the top of the pie.

Cook it in a moderately hot oven - 180°C/350°F - for 20 - 25 minutes until the pastry is crisp and lightly browned.

The pie can be served at once with hot vegetables. Alternatively you can let it cool to room temperature and serve it with a salad.

Chicken with Okra, Chilli and Bananas

Serves 4

A very Caribbean recipe - as good to cool you down on a hot summer evening as to warm you up on a cold winter's night.

60 mL	olive oil	4 tbsp
1	large red pepper, seeded and sliced	1
200 g	okra, topped, tailed and sliced across, thickly	7 oz
1	small fresh or dried red chilli	1
400 g	boned raw chicken, breast or leg	14 oz
450 g	tomatoes, chopped roughly	1 lb
	pinch ground coriander	
1	large banana	1
	salt	
	black pepper	

Heat the oil in a pan and briskly fry the pepper and okra until both are softening. Add the chilli and the cubed chicken and continue to fry briskly until the chicken is lightly browned all over. Add the tomatoes and coriander, cover the dish and cook over a very low

PER SERVING	
Energy Kcals	411.03
Protein g	22.51
Fat g	30.14
Saturated fatty acids g	6.31
Monounsaturated fatty acids g	18.11
Polyunsaturated fatty acids g	4.84
Carbohydrate g	14.14
Total Sugars g	13.17
Sodium mg	282.05
Fibre g	4.19

You could also try using Camargue red rice for this dish. You will get it in delicatessens or health food stores and it is deliciously nutty.

heat for 25 minutes or until the chicken is cooked. If you cook it too quickly the tomatoes will dry up and you will need to add a little water or white wine.

Once the chicken is cooked, add the banana (peeled and sliced thickly), cook for a couple of minutes, then adjust the seasoning to taste. Serve hot with lots of brown rice and a really good green salad.

Chicken Risotto with Fennel and Pine Nuts

Serves 4

This is an excellent way to use up either cooked chicken or turkey. If you do not like coriander, substitute flat-leaved French parsley.

30 mL	olive oil	2 tbsp
2	sticks celery, chopped small	2
250 g	fennel, chopped smallish	9 oz
1	large red pepper, seeded and sliced thinly	1
200 g	brown rice	7 oz
450 mL	water	16 fl oz
150 mL	dry white wine	5 fl oz
200 g	cooked chicken	7 oz
30 mL	pine nuts	2 tbsp
	salt	
	black pepper	
2	sprigs fresh coriander	2

Heat the oil in a heavy pan and add the celery, fennel and pepper. Cook gently until they are beginning to soften, then add the rice. Stir for a minute or two before adding the liquid. Bring to the boil and simmer, uncovered, for 15 minutes. Add the chicken and continue to cook until the liquid is almost evaporated and the rice cooked; add a little more water if necessary. Add the pine nuts and

PER SERVING	
Energy Kcals	456.80
Protein g	21.42
Fat g	19.43
Saturated fatty acids g	3.48
Monounsaturated fatty acids g	10.22
Polyunsaturated fatty acids g	7.54
Carbohydrate g	46.08
Total Sugars g	5.85
Sodium mg	65.28
Fibre g	3.90

If you want to give this dish a Mexican feel, serve it with corn tortillas.

seasoning to taste. Serve warm or cold, generously sprinkled with the chopped coriander.

Chilli Pancakes

Serves 4

This pancake recipe is good for any savoury pancake - and makes for a very filling meal stuffed with chilli con carne!

100 g	chick pea flour	3½ oz
	salt	
200 mL	water	7 fl oz
15 mL	sunflower oil	1 tbsp
1	medium onion, chopped	1
1	medium carrot, scrubbed and diced	1
2	small red chillies, seeded and finely chopped	2
225 g	minced beef	8 oz
50 g	potato flour	2 oz
5 mL, hpd	cayenne pepper	1 hpd tsp
3	medium tomatoes, roughly chopped	3
30 mL	tomato purée	2 tbsp
450 mL	beef or vegetable stock (gluten-free)	16 fl oz
1	tin (425 g) red kidney beans, drained	1
	salt	
	black pepper	

Mix the flour, salt and water in a food processor then allow it to stand for 10 - 15 minutes. You can either make 8 medium-sized,

PER SERVING	
Energy Kcals	389.05
Protein g	27.00
Fat g	11.73
Saturated fatty acids g	3.49
Monounsaturated fatty acids g	4.22
Polyunsaturated fatty acids g	3.93
Carbohydrate g	46.88
Total Sugars g	9.99
Sodium mg	703.65
Fibre g	11.60

A really easy meal for kids when they come home from school - filling and tasty.

thinnish pancakes or four larger, thickish ones. Choose your pan accordingly, then heat a small dribble of oil, just enough to cover the base, and cook the pancakes briskly on either side. Set them aside, interlayered with plastic wrap.

Heat the oil in a pan and briskly fry the onion, carrots and chillies until they are lightly coloured.

Increase the heat and add the meat; fry it rapidly until it is browned, then reduce the heat and add the potato flour mixed with the cayenne pepper. Stir around for a few minutes, then add the tomatoes, tomato purée and the liquid. Bring to the boil and simmer for 15 - 20 minutes. Add the beans and simmer for a further 5 minutes, then adjust the seasoning to taste.

With a slotted spoon remove the meat, vegetables and beans from the pot and use them to fill the pancakes; lay them in a serving dish. Reduce the remaining sauce slightly by boiling it briskly for 4 - 5 minutes, then pour over the pancakes and serve.

"Battered" Meat Loaf

Serves 6

A good old-fashioned way of using up a roast, the "battered" refers to the delicious cheesey batter which is poured over the loaf and makes a crispy crust.

1	egg yolk	1
50 g	sifted chick pea (gram) flour	2 oz
100 mL	water	4 fl oz
350 g	cooked beef	12 oz
150 g	cheddar cheese	5 oz
15 mL	olive oil	1 tbsp
1	medium onion, roughly chopped	1
½	a large cooking apple, peeled and diced	½
15 mL	wholegrain mustard (check ingredients for wheat and gluten)	1 tbsp
5 mL	ground allspice	1 tsp
2	eggs	2
30 mL	low-fat yogurt, gluten free	2 tbsp
	salt and pepper	

Beat the egg yolk, flour and water in a food processor or mixer to make a batter and set aside.

Chop the meat reasonably finely in a processor or mincer and mix it with 4 oz / 100 g of the cheese. Fry the onion in the oil until it is lightly browned and add to the mixture along with the apple, mustard and allspice. Mix the eggs with the yogurt, then mix well into the meat; season lightly.

Form the mixture into a loaf shape on a baking tray or an ovenproof serving dish. Beat half the remaining cheese into the batter and spoon half of this over the loaf. Bake it in a moderately hot oven (190°C / 375°F) for 15 minutes. Remove from the oven, spoon over the rest of the batter, sprinkle the remaining cheese on top and return to the oven for another 15 minutes or until the top is nicely browned. Meanwhile, the extra batter will have dripped down the side and made a crunchy layer around the loaf. The loaf is good either hot or cold.

PER SERVING	
Energy Kcals	329.85
Protein g	29.88
Fat g	18.74
Saturated fatty acids g	8.26
Monounsaturated fatty acids g	7.88
Polyunsaturated fatty acids g	1.59
Carbohydrate g	11.57
Total Sugars g	4.26
Sodium mg	370.18
Fibre g	1.98

If you wanted to prepare this dish well in advance for a party you could cook it to the point where you need to add the snow peas and cream but freeze at that point. When you need to use it, defrost it at room temperature and complete the recipe.

Paprika Beef with Brandy and Cream

Serves 6

A rather rich dish for special occasions; the snow peas give it a lovely crunch.

30 mL	olive oil	2 tbsp
2	medium onions, finely chopped	2
2	cloves garlic, crushed	2
25 g	seasoned potato flour	1 oz
5 mL	paprika	2 tsp
1 kg	lean braising beef, well trimmed of fat and cubed	2 lb 4 oz
30 mL	brandy	2 tbsp
5 mL	dried thyme	1 tsp
2	bay leaves	2
200 g	tomatoes, peeled and chopped roughly	7 oz
300 mL	dry white wine	10 fl oz
200 g	fresh snow peas, halved	7 oz
	salt and pepper	
100 mL	whipping cream	4 fl oz

Heat the oil in a wide pan and gently cook the onion and garlic until they are soft but not coloured. Mix the paprika with the seasoned potato flour and toss the beef cubes thoroughly in it. Add the meat to the onion and garlic and fry briskly until lightly coloured all over. Draw off the heat and cool slightly, then add the brandy and light it. Once the flames have died add the herbs, tomatoes and the wine, making sure that you scrape any burned bits off the bottom of the pan. Bring to the boil, cover and simmer gently for 40 - 50 minutes or until the beef is really tender.

Remove the bay leaves, add the snow peas, continue to cook for a couple of minutes to just take the rawness off the snow peas (they should still be slightly crunchy). Add the cream and adjust the seasoning to taste. Serve at once, decorated with the bay leaves, accompanied by lots of brown rice or baked potatoes.

PER SERVING	
Energy Kcals	471.85
Protein g	51.65
Fat g	20.78
Saturated fatty acids g	8.78
Monounsaturated fatty acids g	10.25
Polyunsaturated fatty acids g	1.36
Carbohydrate g	9.87
Total Sugars g	4.97
Sodium mg	161.34
Fibre g	1.87

Even when cooking for children you can use wine in a casserole - by the time the meat is cooked the alcohol has also been cooked out of the wine, just leaving its flavour behind.

Corn and Beef Hash Casserole

Serves 6

A good filling family casserole which goes down well with children.

500 g	lean ground beef	1 lb 2oz
2	medium onions, finely chopped	2
1	handful fresh parsley, chopped	1
10 mL	dried mixed herbs	2 tsp
	salt and pepper	
100 mL	red wine	4 fl oz
100 mL	water	4 fl oz
15 mL	Worcestershire sauce (gluten free)	1 tbsp
450 g	corn niblets, frozen (defrosted) or tinned (drained)	1 lb
1	medium green pepper, chopped finely	1
4	spring onions, finely chopped	4
1	egg	1
75 g	sifted chick pea (gram) flour	3 oz
75 g	rice flour	3 oz
75 g	low-fat spread	3 oz
45 - 60 mL	water	3 - 4 tbsp

In a bowl mix the beef, onions and herbs and season them lightly. Add the wine, water and Worcestershire sauce and mix thoroughly. Spread half the mixture in the bottom of a pie dish. Mix the corn with the peppers and spring onions and half the egg; spread this over the beef and top with the rest of the meat mixture. Cover the dish with foil or a lid and cook for 30 minutes in a moderate oven (350°F/180°C) or for 10 minutes in a microwave. Remove and cool slightly.

Rub the spread into the flours until they resemble breadcrumbs, then mix to a soft dough with the water. Roll out the pastry and top the pie. Decorate with the trimmings, brush with the rest of the egg and return it to a slightly hotter oven (375°F/190°C) for 25 - 30 minutes or until the pastry is cooked and golden.

Serve with a salad or green vegetables.

PER SERVING	
Energy Kcals	481.20
Protein g	26.07
Fat g	23.11
Saturated fatty acids g	8.14
Monounsaturated fatty acids g	10.37
Polyunsaturated fatty acids g	3.08
Carbohydrate g	41.23
Total Sugars g	5.51
Sodium mg	286.87
Fibre g	5.00

You can use this savoury crumble topping with any other filling you may have.

Beef Crumble

Serves 6

Some people find pastry very time consuming to make so here is a recipe which gives you a topping to your pie without having to make the pastry!

30 mL	sunflower oil	2 tbsp
4	medium leeks, washed and sliced thinly	4
450 g	turnip, peeled and diced	1 lb
40 g	seasoned potato flour (gluten-free)	1½ oz
600 g	lean stewing steak, well trimmed of fat and diced	1 lb 5 oz
300 mL	home-made beef or vegetable stock or water	10 fl oz
100 mL	red wine	4 fl oz
1	bouquet garni	1
	salt and pepper	
125 g	sifted chick pea (gram) flour	4½ oz
125 g	rice flour	4½ oz
60 g	butter or low-fat spread	2 oz
60 g	grated cheddar cheese	2 oz

Heat the oil in a pan and cook the leeks and turnip fairly briskly until they are lightly browned all over. Toss the beef in the seasoned flour, then add it to the pan and continue to cook until the beef is brown. Add the stock and wine, stir around well, add the bouquet garni and cook very slowly on the stove top or in a moderate oven (180°C / 350°F) for an hour or until the beef is really tender. Adjust the seasoning to taste and turn into a pie dish.

Rub the butter or low-fat spread and cheese into the flours as for a pastry, and when they are well mixed spread the mixture over the beef. Put it back in the oven for a further 30 minutes to cook and crisp the top. Serve at once with a green vegetable.

PER SERVING	
Energy Kcals	454.48
Protein g	33.47
Fat g	17.9
Saturated fatty acids g	6.22
Monounsaturated fatty acids g	7.04
Polyunsaturated fatty acids g	5.44
Carbohydrate g	37.85
Total Sugars g	5.97
Sodium mg	291.36
Fibre g	5.92

Long slow cooking will give flavour to any dish. A slow cooker, if you enjoy well-flavoured casseroles, might be a good investment.

Filet de Boeuf a L'Italienne

Serves 8

A splendid Victorian beef dish to serve for a dinner party - the bacon and the long slow cooking give the beef an excellent flavour.

3 kg	beef sirloin roast	6 lb 8 oz
50 g	mushrooms, chopped very finely	2 oz
2	handfuls of fresh parsley	2
1/2	a medium onion, finely chopped	1/2
	freshly ground black pepper	
2	thick slices of back bacon	2
25 g	butter	1 oz
2.5 mL	dried marjoram	1/2 tsp
2.5 mL	dried thyme	1/2 tsp
	grated peel of 1 lime or small lemon	
1	clove garlic, crushed	1
1	medium onion, finely chopped	1
100 g	carrot, diced finely	4 oz
30 mL	tomato purée	2 tbsp
600 mL	water or home-made beef, veal or vegetable stock	1 pint
225 g	wheat- and gluten-free macaroni	8 oz
15 mL	finely grated cheddar cheese	1 tbsp

Heat the oven to 150°C / 300°F .

Mix the chopped mushrooms, parsley, onion and pepper into a paste and coat the slices of bacon. Cut an incision the length of the beef, lay in the coated bacon and tie the meat back into shape. Heat the butter in a heavy pan large enough to hold the beef and gently cook the herbs, peel, garlic, onion and carrot for 10 minutes. Place the meat on top of the vegetables. Mix the tomato purée with the stock and pour around the meat. Cover and cook very slowly, in the oven or on the stove top, for 3 hours.

When you are ready to serve the meat, cook the macaroni according to the instructions on the package. Drain it thoroughly

PER SERVING	
Energy Kcals	641.15
Protein g	93.20
Fat g	19.63
Saturated fatty acids g	8.84
Monounsaturated fatty acids g	8.18
Polyunsaturated fatty acids g	1.75
Carbohydrate g	24.87
Total Sugars g	3.33
Sodium mg	542.92
Fibre g	1.95

Try the steak and kidney pie cold with salad. Although cold meat pies have rather gone out of fashion they were great favourites with our grandparents - who knew a thing or two about good food.

and return it to the pan. Remove the meat onto a large warmed serving dish and remove its ties. Adjust the seasoning of the cooking juices to taste and add them, along with the vegetables and the grated cheese, to the macaroni. Mix all well together and spoon it around the beef. To serve, slice the beef and serve it with the macaroni and vegetables.

Steak and Kidney Pie

Serves 6

An old favourite often off the menu for wheat and gluten allergic people. The pie freezes well in its dish topped with pastry, either cooked or uncooked; if uncooked, take care not to burn the pastry when reheating it.

150 g	sifted gram /chick pea flour	5 oz
75 g	low-fat spread	3 oz
750 g	stewing steak, well trimmed and diced	1 lb 10 oz
450 g	pork kidney, trimmed and diced	1 lb
350 g	button mushrooms, wiped and halved if they are very large	12 oz
50 g	potato flour	2 oz
	salt and pepper	
	water	
1	egg	1

Heat the oven to 180°C / 350°F .

Rub the spread into the gram flour until it is crumbly, then mix to a paste with approximately 45 mL / 3 tablespoons water. Set aside in the fridge.

Mix the trimmed, cubed steak with the kidney and the mushrooms. Season the potato flour, then toss the meats and the mushrooms in the flour until all the pieces are well covered. Turn them into a pie dish, sprinkle over any remaining flour and fill the

PER SERVING	
Energy Kcals	464.12
Protein g	46.22
Fat g	23.15
Saturated fatty acids g	8.21
Monounsaturated fatty acids g	10.51
Polyunsaturated fatty acids g	3.05
Carbohydrate g	19.1
Total Sugars g	1.15
Sodium mg	537.4
Fibre g	3.79

dish ⅔ of the way up with cold water. Cover it with foil or a lid and cook it for about 1 hour or until the steak is tender. Take it out of the oven after half an hour and stir around to make sure the flour is well mixed in.

Roll out the pastry and top the pie (supporting the middle with an egg cup if the dish is rather large for the filling). Decorate the top with the pastry trimmings and brush with the beaten egg.

Return to the oven for 25 - 30 minutes or until the crust is cooked and lightly browned. The pie can be eaten hot with vegetables or cold with baked potatoes and a salad.

Cassoulet

Serves 6

Another classic and substantial dish normally barred to those allergic to wheat or gluten. Make sure you push the bread slices well down into the casserole so that they absorb the juices.

300 g	dried haricot beans	12 oz
4	slices of bacon	4
2	carrots , scrubbed and sliced	2
2	onions stuck with 10 cloves, plus 2 large onions, chopped roughly	2
4	cloves garlic, halved	4
10	peppercorns	10
	salt	
25 g	butter	1 oz
150 g	garlic sausages, diced	6 oz
500 g	leg or shoulder of lamb, trimmed of fat and cubed	1 lb
30 mL	tomato purée	2 tbsp
800 mL	water or home-made chicken or vegetable stock	25 fl oz
2	slices of gluten- and wheat-free white or wholemeal bread	2
30 mL	wholegrain or Dijon mustard (check ingredients list for wheat and gluten)	2 tbsp

Soak the beans in cold water for a minimum of 4 hours, then drain and discard the water. Line a casserole big enough to hold all the ingredients with the bacon slices. In a bowl mix together the beans, carrots, onions stuck with cloves, 2 cloves of garlic, the peppercorns and salt. Spoon this mixture into the pot with the bacon, just cover it with water and bake it, covered, in a moderately cool oven (160°C/325°F) for 2 hours.

Meanwhile, melt the butter in a heavy-based pan and brown the garlic sausage and the lamb. Stir in the chopped onion, the rest of the garlic, the tomato purée and the stock. Bring to the boil and simmer gently for 30 minutes.

Turn the meat mixture into the bean pot, stir all well together and return to the oven for another 30 minutes. Taste and adjust the seasoning if necessary.

Spread the pieces of bread on one side with the mustard. Lay them on top of the casserole, mustard side up, and push them down so that the bottom of each slice absorbs the juices. Return the casserole to the oven for 20 - 25 minutes to heat and crisp the topping.

Serve at once with plenty of green vegetables or a salad.

PER SERVING	
Energy Kcals	542.64
Protein g	38.19
Fat g	30.26
Saturated fatty acids g	13.68
Monounsaturated fatty acids g	13.62
Polyunsaturated fatty acids g	2.91
Carbohydrate g	31.44
Total Sugars g	9.67
Sodium mg	945.5
Fibre g	6.17

Right:
Pancakes (page 147)

Even though it is almost impossible to buy anything other than lamb these days - mutton is an endangered species - there is still something rather special about the first young lambs around Easter. Well worth a special effort.

Spring Lamb en Croute

Serves 6

The gram flour makes a delicious but crumbly pastry. When it goes in the oven the sides may "slither" down to the base leaving your en croute with a hat rather than totally covered but it looks quite attractive and tastes delicious.

150 g	gram or chick pea flour	5 oz
75 g	low-fat spread or butter	3 oz
1 kg	boned and rolled leg or shoulder of lamb	2 lb 4 oz
4	cloves garlic, peeled but left whole	4
45 mL	olive oil	3 tbsp
100 g	button mushrooms, chopped finely in a food processor	4 oz
20 g	sun-dried tomatoes, soaked if necessary, and chopped finely	3/4 oz
	large handful of fresh parsley, finely chopped	

Put the gram flour into a bowl and cut in the spread or butter. Crumble with your fingers until the mixture is like fine sand, then add 60 - 90 mL / 4-6 tablespoons water to make a softish dough. Cover and put in the fridge to chill.

Cut three or four slits in the lamb and insert the garlic. Cover the lamb with a piece of foil and bake in a moderate oven (180°C/350°F) for 40 minutes. Remove and allow to partially cool.

Meanwhile, heat the oil and sweat the mushrooms with the sun-dried tomatoes, covered, for 10 - 15 minutes. Add the finely chopped parsley.

To finish reheat the oven to 180°C/350°F. Roll out the pastry to a large enough square to cover the lamb.

Spread the mushroom mixture over the top of the lamb, then carefully cover the lamb with the pastry, tucking it in around the bottom of the roast. Decorate with spare scraps of pastry.

Return to the oven and bake for 20 - 25 minutes or until the pastry is crisp and lightly browned. Serve at once with lots of fresh vegetables.

PER SERVING	
Energy Kcals	544.44
Protein g	38.36
Fat g	37.94
Saturated fatty acids g	13.15
Monounsaturated fatty acids g	17.24
Polyunsaturated fatty acids g	4.72
Carbohydrate g	13.37
Total Sugars g	.99
Sodium mg	241.75
Fibre g	3.20

Left:
Carrot and Ginger Tart
(page 144)

The combination of apples, onions and meat is a very familiar one in English cookery - a Devon Lamb Casserole, for example, uses ham instead of lamb or mutton but is in other respects very similar to this one.

Lamb Casserole

Serves 6

The Lamb Casserole is quite sweet because of the apples and the cider but the sweetness complements the meat.

15 mL	sunflower oil	1 tbsp
1	large onion, peeled and sliced	1
150 g	cooking apple, peeled, cored and sliced	5 oz
450 g	mature lamb, trimmed of fat and cubed	1 lb
15 g	dark brown sugar	½ oz
10 mL	dried thyme	2 tsp
150 mL	dry cider	5 fl oz
175 g	chick pea (gram) flour	6 oz
75 g	butter	3 oz
	water	
1	egg	1
	salt and pepper	

Heat the oven to 180°C/350°F.

Pour the oil into the base of a round or oval pie dish and lay half the onion mixed with half the apple in the bottom. Trim the meat and cut it into 2.5 cm / 1 inch cubes. Season it well and mix it with the thyme and the sugar. Lay the meat over the apples and onions and cover it with the rest of the apple and onion mixture. Pour in the cider and cover the pie with foil.

Bake it for around 40 minutes or until the lamb is nearly cooked. Transfer to a smaller dish or put a pie support in the middle of the dish.

Meanwhile make the pastry by rubbing the butter into the gram flour until it is sandy then mixing to a soft dough with 45 - 60 mL / 2-3 tablespoons of water.

When the filling is ready, roll out the pastry. Cut a rim of pastry to go round the pie dish. Wet the rim of the dish with a little water to make the pastry stick, then wet the pastry rim to make the lid stick. Cover the pie, pressing down the edges with your fingers. Decorate the lid with the pastry trimmings (in balls or leaves) and brush generously with the beaten egg. Bake for 30 minutes or until the pastry is cooked and golden. Serve hot or warm with new potatoes and a green vegetable.

PER SERVING	
Energy Kcals	416.74
Protein g	29.8
Fat g	23.59
Saturated fatty acids g	12.29
Monounsaturated fatty acids g	7.03
Polyunsaturated fatty acids g	3.23
Carbohydrate g	21.63
Total Sugars g	7.19
Sodium mg	256.68
Fibre g	3.75

A rack of lamb is also excellent cooked on a barbecue. If you wish to do that, sit the lamb on a branch of fresh rosemary which will not only flavour the lamb but scent it.

Rack of Lamb with Mustard Crust

Serves 6

The mustard crust gives an excellent flavour to the lamb. Serve with fresh green vegetables such as broccoli, spinach or green beans.

	Rack of lamb with at least 12 cutlets, trimmed of most of its fat	
Crust		
15 mL	sunflower oil	1 tbsp
60 mL	wholegrain mustard - check to make sure it does not contain wheat starch or gluten	4 tbsp
25 g	finely chopped parsley	1 oz
100 g	shallots, very finely chopped	4 oz
15 mL	dried rosemary	1 tbsp
5 mL	dried marjoram	1 tsp
5 mL	dried oregano	1 tsp
5 mL	dried thyme	1 tsp
45 mL	dry white wine	3 tbsp
1	small package plain potato chips (gluten free)	1

Heat the oven to 180°C/350°F.

Roast the rack of lamb uncovered in a baking tray for 15 minutes per 500 g - this will give a moderately pink middle. If you want it more cooked, then cook it for 20 minutes per 500 g.

Meanwhile combine all the crust ingredients apart from the chips. Crush the chips in a plastic bag with a rolling pin.

About 10 minutes before the meat is ready, take it out of the oven and spread the fat side with a thick layer of the mustard mixture. Sprinkle over the crushed chips and return it to the oven for the last 10 minutes to finish cooking the meat and crisp the crust.

PER SERVING	
Energy Kcals	305.45
Protein g	29.48
Fat g	18.00
Saturated fatty acids g	6.91
Monounsaturated fatty acids g	6.60
Polyunsaturated fatty acids g	3.00
Carbohydrate g	5.40
Total Sugars g	1.50
Sodium mg	294.11
Fibre g	1.18

This curry mixture also works well with pork or chicken.

Curried Lamb with Greek Yogurt

Serves 6

Like most curries the flavour will mature if you can make the dish the day before you want to eat it, leave it in the fridge overnight, then reheat it to serve. If you intend to do this, do not add the yogurt until just before serving the dish.

30 mL	sunflower oil	2 tbsp
2	medium onions, peeled and finely chopped	2
3	large cloves garlic, peeled and finely chopped	3
25 g	ginger root , peeled and finely chopped	1 oz
5 mL, hpd	ground cumin	1 hpd tsp
30 mL, hpd	medium curry powder (check to make sure it does not contain any wheat or gluten)	6 hpd tsp
200 g	zucchini, topped and tailed and sliced	7 oz
100 g	green beans, topped and tailed and sliced	4 oz
400 g	tomatoes, fresh (peeled and quartered) or tinned (chopped)	14 oz
400 g	cooked lamb, trimmed of any fat and diced	14 oz
400 mL	water	14 fl oz
200 g	cooking apples, peeled, cored and diced	7 oz
50 g	raisins	2 oz
	juice of 2 large lemons	
100 mL	Marsala or medium sherry	3½ fl oz
200 g	Greek yogurt, gluten free	7 oz
	salt and black pepper	

PER SERVING	
Energy Kcals	315.85
Protein g	17.89
Fat g	18.32
Saturated fatty acids g	7.47
Monounsaturated fatty acids g	6.98
Polyunsaturated fatty acids g	4.28
Carbohydrate g	17.48
Total Sugars g	14.62
Sodium mg	172.45
Fibre g	3.61

Heat the oil in a deep wide pan and add the onion, garlic, ginger root and spices. Cook them all together gently for 5 - 10 minutes then add the vegetables, the cooked lamb, the apple and the water. Bring to the boil, then cover and simmer very gently for 30 - 40 minutes. Add the raisins, lemon juice and Marsala or sherry and continue to cook, scarcely even simmering for a further 10 minutes. Finally add the yogurt and season to taste. Serve with plenty of rice and a green salad.

Bobotie

Serves 6

This is a classic South African dish which, in the original, uses breadcrumbs with the lamb. However, lentils make an excellent substitute. It can be eaten hot or cold.

1 kg	1 medium-sized lean leg of lamb	2 lb 4 oz
100 g	brown lentils	3½ oz
600 mL	milk	1 pint
30 mL	olive or sunflower oil	2 tbsp
2	medium onions, chopped	2
30 mL	medium curry powder	2 tbsp
	juice of 2 lemons	
	salt and pepper	
3	medium eggs	3
200 mL	milk	7 fl oz
50 g	chopped almonds	2 oz
75 g	raisins	3 oz

Put the leg of lamb into a heavy ovenproof casserole with the brown lentils and the milk. Cover the pot tightly and cook in a moderate oven (180°C/350°F) or on a low heat on the stove top for approximately 1 hour or until the lamb and lentils are cooked and most of the milk absorbed.

Remove the lamb from the pot, remove the meat from the bones and mince it in a food processor. Mix the minced lamb with the lentils and any remaining milk.

Heat the oil in a heavy pan and add the onions and curry powder. Cook them together gently for around 5 minutes, then mix them into the lamb and lentils along with the lemon juice and a little seasoning. Spoon this mixture into an ovenproof casserole and flatten it out.

Beat the eggs with the milk, then add the almonds and the raisins. Pour this mixture over the lamb and return the dish, uncovered, to the oven for a further 30 minutes or until the top is lightly browned and puffed.

Serve with plenty of light and crunchy salads.

PER SERVING	
Energy Kcals	627.17
Protein g	63.87
Fat g	30.1
Saturated fatty acids g	10.89
Monounsaturated fatty acids g	14.21
Polyunsaturated fatty acids g	4.17
Carbohydrate g	27.66
Total Sugars g	18.3
Sodium mg	311.24
Fibre g	3.22

Beans are particularly good with relatively fatty meats such as lamb or pork as they absorb the fat thus making it more digestible.

Leg of Lamb Casserole with Beans and Green Peppercorns

Serves 8

Because the garlic is cooked long and slowly with the lamb its flavour is quite mild. Indeed, the whole cloves have been mistaken for cannellini beans!

10	large cloves garlic, peeled but left whole	10
2 kg	lean leg of lamb	4 lb 8 oz
60 mL	olive oil	4 tbsp
400 g	fresh spinach, washed and lightly dried, or frozen spinach, defrosted and well drained	14 oz
400 g	tinned flageolet beans*, drained	14 oz
400 g	tinned cannellini beans*, drained	14 oz
2	large sprigs fresh rosemary or 2 teaspoons dried	2
	handful of green peppercorns	

Insert 6 garlic cloves into the lamb, then put the rest into a heavy casserole dish (one that you can use on the stove top) with the oil and the spinach. Cook briskly for 4 -5 minutes or until the spinach is wilted. Add the beans, rosemary and green peppercorns.

Lay the leg of lamb on top of the vegetables and beans and cover the casserole tightly. The dish can then be cooked very slowly either on the stove top on in a low oven (150˚C/300˚F) for 3 - 4 hours.

To serve, remove the lamb from the casserole onto a serving dish and surround with the spinach and bean mixture.

* If you cannot find these products, use red kidney beans and white kidney beans respectively.

PER SERVING	
Energy Kcals	645.8
Protein g	82.64
Fat g	28.81
Saturated fatty acids g	10.96
Monounsaturated fatty acids g	13.39
Polyunsaturated fatty acids g	2.41
Carbohydrate g	14.70
Total Sugars g	1.70
Sodium mg	593.14
Fibre g	6.21

If you have time and think about it in advance you can cook your own beans but I find that the small extra expense in buying canned beans is greatly outweighed by their convenience.

Leg of Lamb with Zucchini and Lima Beans

Serves 6

Beans make particularly good casseroled dishes as they absorb the flavours to produce a delicious, easy-to-cook, all-in-one meal.

6	cloves of garlic	6
30 mL	olive oil	2 tbsp
500 g	zucchini	1 lb 2 oz
500 g	tinned lima beans, drained	1 lb 2 oz
2	large sprigs fresh rosemary	2
1.5 kg	lean leg of lamb	3 lb 5 oz

Peel the garlic cloves, then put them, whole, into a heavy oven-proof casserole large enough to fit the lamb, along with the oil, zucchini, lima beans and rosemary. Sit the leg of lamb on top of them.

Cover the casserole tightly and cook very slowly - either on very low heat on the stove top or in a very low oven (130°C/ 250°F) - for 3 - 4 hours. Alternatively you could cook it in a slow cooker. The zucchini and lamb should produce enough moisture for you not to need any extra liquid but check halfway through the cooking and if it looks a little dry add 200 mL/7 fl oz of water or vegetable stock.

At the end of the cooking time the lamb should be very tender and the flavours all deliciously amalgamated. It should not need any extra seasoning.

PER SERVING	
Energy Kcals	608.17
Protein g	80.39
Fat g	26.10
Saturated fatty acids g	10.62
Monounsaturated fatty acids g	12.70
Polyunsaturated fatty acids g	1.91
Carbohydrate g	13.37
Total Sugars g	2.41
Sodium mg	518.83
Fibre g	4.79

There was a time when you would have needed to salt your eggplants and leave them to drain for some hours to remove their bitterness. However, thanks to modern breeding techniques you can now use them straight from your shopping basket.

Alternative Moussaka

Serves 6

The hummus and Parmesan make a very rich but delicious topping for the moussaka.

30 mL	olive oil	2 tbsp
2	large eggplants, sliced	2
300 g	lean cooked lamb, diced	10 oz
350 g	tomatoes, sliced	12 oz
	salt and pepper	
5 mL, hpd	dried marjoram	1 hpd tsp
300 mL	Greek yogurt (gluten free)	10 fl oz
300 g	hummus - check ingredients to make sure they do not include wheat starch or gluten	10 oz
75 g	grated fresh Parmesan	3 oz

Fry the eggplant slices in the oil until they are lightly browned on each side. Lay half of them out in the bottom of an ovenproof casserole. Lay the lamb over the eggplant and cover it with the sliced tomato. Sprinkle this with salt and pepper and the marjoram. Cover with the remains of the eggplant. Mix the yogurt with the hummus and Parmesan and season it lightly, then spoon the mixture over the eggplant. Cook in a moderate oven (180 °C / 350°F) for 20 - 30 minutes or until the top is well browned. Serve at once.

PER SERVING	
Energy Kcals	363.17
Protein g	23.18
Fat g	24.78
Saturated fatty acids g	8.75
Monounsaturated fatty acids g	12.35
Polyunsaturated fatty acids g	2.62
Carbohydrate g	13.03
Total Sugars g	4.8
Sodium mg	453.8
Fibre g	4.30

If your butcher will make you gluten- or wheat-free sausages, make sure that he really understands about contamination.

Pork Sausages

Serves 8

If you have a local butcher he may well be prepared to make you sausages without gluten.

250 g	well-trimmed pork fillet or shoulder	9 oz
2	slices bacon	2
75 g	wheat- and gluten-free bread crumbs	3 oz
50 g	onion	2 oz
5 mL	salt	1 tsp
2.5 mL	black pepper	½ tsp
2.5 mL	ground nutmeg	½ tsp
5 mL	Worcestershire sauce (gluten free)	1 tsp

Put all the ingredients into a food processor or through a mincer so that they are well amalgamated.

Form the mixture into 8 fat or 12 thinner sausages. You can roll them in some extra breadcrumbs if you wish. Grill or shallow fry for 4 - 5 minutes and serve with mashed potatoes or whatever else you would normally serve with sausages.

PER SERVING	
Energy Kcals	112.75
Protein g	9.06
Fat g	5.43
Saturated fatty acids g	1.78
Monounsaturated fatty acids g	1.93
Polyunsaturated fatty acids g	.70
Carbohydrate g	7.42
Total Sugars g	0.54
Sodium mg	362.20
Fibre g	0.73

People always assume that sausages have to have skins but skins are really quite unnecessary.

Pork Sausages with Polenta

Serves 8

250 g	well-trimmed pork fillet / shoulder	9 oz
1	slice bacon	1
1	small onion	1
50 g	coarse polenta / maize meal	2 oz
150 mL	water	5 fl oz
25 g	chick pea (gram) flour	1 oz
5 mL	salt	1 tsp
2.5 mL	black pepper	½ tsp
2.5 mL	ground nutmeg	½ tsp
1 tsp	Worcestershire sauce (gluten free)	1 tsp

Mix the diced, trimmed pork with the bacon and the onion in a food processor or a mincer. Meanwhile bring the water to the boil in a small saucepan, then add the polenta. Cook gently, stirring continually for several minutes or until the polenta has fully absorbed the water and thickened somewhat. Beat the polenta into the minced pork along with the gram flour, salt, pepper, nutmeg and Worcestershire sauce.

Form the mixture into 8 fat sausages. To stop them being too sticky you can roll them in a little extra gram or rice flour. Broil or shallow fry for 4 - 5 minutes or until you are sure they are cooked through but take care in turning them as the sausages are quite soft, and of course, have no skins so can fall apart quite easily.

Serve with mashed potatoes or whatever else you would normally serve with sausages.

PER SERVING	
Energy Kcals	93.72
Protein g	8.64
Fat g	3.74
Saturated fatty acids g	1.30
Monounsaturated fatty acids g	1.39
Polyunsaturated fatty acids g	.64
Carbohydrate g	6.61
Total Sugars g	.520
Sodium mg	314.45
Fibre g	.42

Chicory can be quite bitter if you eat it raw. However, blanching for just a few seconds in boiling water takes the real bitterness out leaving just enough sharpness to counteract the relative blandness of a white sauce.

Ham and Chicory Stuffed Pancakes

Serves 4

A gluten- and wheat-free version of a classic Belgian dish. The pancakes can be used with any other savoury filling.

100 g	chick pea (gram) flour	4 oz
	small pinch salt	
200 mL	water	7 fl oz
30 mL	sunflower oil	2 tbsp
1	medium onion, chopped	1
1	large head chicory (Belgian endive), sliced thickly across the head	1
25 g	potato flour	1 oz
350 mL	milk	12 fl oz
100 g	well-flavoured ham, chopped into matchsticks	4 oz
	salt and black pepper	
	handful of fresh parsley chopped	

Whizz the gram flour, salt and water in a food processor, then allow to stand for 10 - 15 minutes. Heat a pancake pan with a tiny dribble of oil. Pour one small ladleful of the mixture into the pan and cook quickly on both sides. The pancakes should be quite thin and you should get four out of the mixture with a couple left over for tasting. Set them aside with a layer of plastic wrap or greaseproof paper between each pancake.

Heat the rest of the sunflower oil in a shallow pan and cook the onion until just beginning to soften. Meanwhile blanch the chopped chicory in boiling water for 2 minutes only and drain. When the onion is soft, add the potato flour off the heat, stir well, then gradually, still off the heat, add the milk and stir until the sauce is quite smooth. Return to the heat and continue to stir until the sauce thickens. Add the ham and chicory and continue to cook for a couple of minutes to allow the flavours to amalgamate. Season lightly to taste with salt and pepper then add the chopped parsley.

Arrange the pancakes either flat on a plate with a layer of the

PER SERVING	
Energy Kcals	304.20
Protein g	15.08
Fat g	17.29
Saturated fatty acids g	5.29
Monounsaturated fatty acids g	5.46
Polyunsaturated fatty acids g	6.14
Carbohydrate g	24.10
Total Sugars g	6.67
Sodium mg	399.25
Fibre g	3.79

filling in between each pancake to make a "cake", or fill each pancake with the filling and fold them over. You can arrange them on one big plate or on four individual plates. Cover with plastic wrap and reheat for 2½ minutes each for the individual pancakes / about 6 minutes for the cake in a microwave on High. Alternatively, cover tightly with aluminum foil and reheat in a moderate oven for about 30 minutes before serving.

Sweet and Sour Pork

Serves 4

The cornstarch makes a delicious crisp batter for this Chinese flavoured pork dish. Excellent with lots of fluffy white rice.

400 g	pork fillet , trimmed and cubed	14 oz
1	small egg, beaten	1
50 g	cornstarch, seasoned	2 oz
	vegetable oil for deep frying plus 30 mL / 2 tbsp corn oil	
10 mL	potato flour	2 tsp
60 mL	water	4 tbsp
60 mL	rice or wine vinegar	2½ fl oz
60 mL	light brown sugar	4 tbsp
1 mL	salt	½ tsp
30 mL	tomato purée	2 tbsp
10 mL	Worcestershire sauce (gluten free)	2 tsp
1	clove garlic, peeled and chopped finely	1
1	medium onion, finely chopped	1
1	medium green pepper, seeded and chopped	1
100 g	tinned pineapple chunks, with their juice (not syrup)	4 oz

Make sure the pork is well trimmed, then toss it in the egg and dredge it in the seasoned cornstarch, making sure that every piece is well covered.

Half fill a wok or deep fryer with oil and heat it until a piece of stale wheat- and gluten-free bread browns in one minute. Deep fry the pork pieces, for approximately 1 minute, making sure that they stay separate, then drain on paper towels.

Dissolve the potato flour in the water and 60 mL / 4 tablespoons of juice from the pineapple. Add the vinegar, sugar, salt, tomato purée and Worcestershire sauce and mix well together.

Heat 15 mL / 1 tablespoon of the oil in a frying pan and when it is hot add the garlic and onion, stir it around for a little, then add the green pepper. Stir fry for a couple of minutes, season lightly, then add the pineapple chunks. Pour in the sauce and bring to the boil, stirring continuously.

Reheat the deep frying oil until a piece of bread browns in 50 seconds. Refry the pork pieces for 2 - 3 minutes to ensure that the outside is crisp without letting the inside dry up. Drain on paper towels and keep warm.

Reheat the sweet and sour sauce and stir in the remaining oil. Pour over the pork and serve at once.

PER SERVING	
Energy Kcals	492.07
Protein g	25.23
Fat g	27.12
Saturated fatty acids g	6.06
Monounsaturated fatty acids g	8.26
Polyunsaturated fatty acids g	12.48
Carbohydrate g	41.05
Total Sugars g	27.33
Sodium mg	234.68
Fibre g	1.46

Pork Fillet with Artichokes and Orange

Serves 6

Both pork and lamb fillets are rather under-rated cuts of meat which is surprising as they are so flexible. Moreover, since there is virtually no waste, they are a lot more economical than a cut where half of it may turn out to be gristle and fat.

750 g	pork fillet, trimmed of fat and slit open	1 lb 10 oz
450 g	Jerusalem artichokes, scrubbed, trimmed and sliced thinly	1 lb
100 g	broken walnuts	4 oz
30 mL	olive oil	2 tbsp
2	garlic cloves, crushed	2
2	medium onions, finely chopped	2

1	medium cooking apple, peeled and sliced thinly	1
300 mL	dry white wine	10 fl oz
300 mL	water or home-made chicken or vegetable stock	10 fl oz
	freshly squeezed juice of 2 oranges	

Open out the pork fillet, sprinkle it lightly with salt and pepper and lay slices of artichoke and walnuts down the middle. You should have some walnuts left over; toss these in a little oil and set them aside. You may find it easier to cut the fillet in two completely so as to get the filling well distributed. Tie it into a neat sausage.

Melt the rest of the oil in a heavy pan and fry the pork roll briskly until it is lightly browned on each side. Reduce the heat and add the garlic and onion; continue to cook until they soften without turning colour, then add the rest of the artichokes, apple and the liquids. Cover the pan and simmer for 50 - 60 minutes or until the pork is quite tender.

Remove the pork from the casserole, cut the strings and slice the sausage neatly. Lay the slices on a warmed serving dish. Adjust the seasoning to taste and spoon the vegetables and sauce over the pork. Decorate with the remains of the walnuts and serve with brown rice and a green vegetable or salad.

PER SERVING	
Energy Kcals	439.25
Protein g	31.98
Fat g	24.91
Saturated fatty acids g	6.26
Monounsaturated fatty acids g	10.19
Polyunsaturated fatty acids g	11.11
Carbohydrate g	16.26
Total Sugars g	8.38
Sodium mg	73.62
Fibre g	4.31

This dish can easily be cooked in advance, then heated in a microwave before serving.

Cauliflower Cheese with Bacon and Green Peas

Serves 4

Cauliflower cheese is so popular as a dish with both adults and children that it is worth working out some variations on that theme. You can use either old or new potatoes for this and fresh or frozen peas.

400 g	potatoes , scrubbed and cubed	14 oz
400 g	cauliflower	14 oz
200 g	peas, fresh or frozen	7 oz
100 g	lean bacon slices,	3½ oz
25 g	butter or low-fat spread	1 oz

25 g	cornstarch	1 oz
450 mL	2% milk	16 fl oz
100 g	Boursin or other soft herbed cheese	3½ oz

Scrub the potatoes and quarter them, then steam them for 15 minutes or until they are nearly cooked. Cut the cauliflower into florets and add it to the steamer. Continue to steam for another 5 minutes or until the cauliflower is nearly cooked, then add the peas to the steamer. Continue to steam for a further 3 minutes.

Fry the bacon until crisp, remove any excess fat, and chop into small pieces.

Melt the butter or low-fat spread and stir in the cornstarch. Gradually add the milk, stirring all the time, over a low heat, until the sauce thickens. Add the herbed cheese and season to taste.

When ready to serve, decant the vegetables and the bacon pieces into the sauce. Mix gently together, then turn into a serving dish and serve at once.

PER SERVING	
Energy Kcals	433.44
Protein g	18.96
Fat g	24.81
Saturated fatty acids g	13.84
Monounsaturated fatty acids g	8.77
Polyunsaturated fatty acids g	2.39
Carbohydrate g	35.86
Total Sugars g	9.73
Sodium mg	599.88
Fibre g	5.66

Games birds are relatively expensive as, unlike poultry, they are not intensively reared. None the less, they are worth the occasional splash out as they do have a flavour you will never get from a domestically reared bird.

Pheasant Braised with White Grapes

Serves 6

This is a very easy way to cook pheasants as it guarantees that they do not dry out, while giving them an excellent flavour. Fresh pheasant are usually only available during the winter but you may find frozen ones year round.

2	large pheasants, trussed	2
50 g	butter	2 oz
12	spring onions bulbs, finely chopped	12
2	sprigs rosemary	2
450 mL	dry white wine	16 fl oz
	salt and pepper	
225 g	seedless white grapes, halved	8 oz

PER SERVING	
Energy Kcals	566
Protein g	68.2
Fat g	25.26
Saturated fatty acids g	10.65
Monounsaturated fatty acids g	11.37
Polyunsaturated fatty acids g	2.91
Carbohydrate g	6.73
Total Sugars g	6.59
Sodium mg	339.24
Fibre g	.45

Remember that duck, like goose, is a very rich meat so a little goes a very long way.

In a heavy casserole fry the pheasants briskly on all sides in the butter until they are well bronzed all over. Add the onions, reduce the heat and continue to fry more gently until the onions soften. Add the rosemary, wine and a little salt and pepper, cover the casserole and cook gently on the stove top or in a moderate oven (160°C / 325°F) for 1 hour.

Take out of the oven. Remove the pheasants onto a warmed serving dish, cover and keep warm. Remove the rosemary from the cooking juices, add the grapes and continue to simmer on the stove top for a further couple of minutes to warm the grapes through.

Adjust the seasoning to taste and spoon the grapes and cooking juices around the pheasants. If there is too much to fit, serve the rest in a sauce boat or jug.

Serve with new potatoes or brown rice and a green vegetable or a salad.

Duck with Apple and Orange Sauce

Serves 6

A rather less rich version of the classic Duck à l'Orange which is given a nice tang by the orange rind.

1	large duck	1
1	small cooking apple	1
1	medium onion	1
1	stick celery	1
1	tomato	1
1	sprig parsley	1
150 mL	red wine	5 fl oz
300 mL	water	10 fl oz
	rind and juice of 2 oranges	
15 g	butter	½ oz
15 g	potato flour	½ oz
	salt and pepper	

Heat the oven to 180°C / 350°F .

Prick the duck's skin thoroughly, fill its cavity with the cooking apple, peeled and chopped roughly and roast it for about 1½ hours. Meanwhile, make some good stock from the giblets of the duck (reserving the liver) by bringing them to the boil, along with the onion, celery and tomato in 15 mL / 1 tablespoon of sunflower oil, parsley, wine, water and a little seasoning, then simmering them for 30 - 45 minutes.

Carefully peel the rind off the oranges, taking as little pith as possible. Cut it in thin matchsticks and blanch it for a couple of minutes in boiling water.

When the duck is cooked, remove it from the rack and pour off as much of the fat in the roasting tin as you possibly can. A jug with an upper and lower spout is very useful for this.

Melt the butter in a saucepan, add the duck liver chopped small and cook for a couple of minutes. Add the potato flour, stir well and cook another minute or two, then add the juices from the pan, the apple from the middle of the duck, well mushed up, 300 mL/ 10 fl oz of the strained stock and the juice from the 2 oranges. Stir well, bring to the boil and simmer for 5 - 10 minutes. Meanwhile, carve the duck and lay it in a warmed serving dish, removing as much or as little of the fatty (but crisp) skin as you want. Strain the sauce, return it to the pan, add the orange rinds and reheat. Adjust the seasoning to taste and pour it over the duck. Serve at once with green vegetables and really baby new potatoes, if they are available.

PER SERVING	
Energy Kcals	225.02
Protein g	25.57
Fat g	8.54
Saturated fatty acids g	3.94
Monounsaturated fatty acids g	4.73
Polyunsaturated fatty acids g	1.25
Carbohydrate g	8.66
Total Sugars g	6.44
Sodium mg	234.25
Fibre g	1.07

Squab can be very tough if just plain roasted so it is always better to casserole them or to use their flesh in a composite dish such as this risotto.

Risotto of Squab and Wild Rice

Serves 6

This rather exotic risotto is based on a sixteenth-century Italian dish which was served covered in sliced truffles. Since truffles are hideously expensive, I have introduced some wild rice and seaweed instead!

2-4	small onions or 4 shallots, finely chopped	2-4
100 g	mushrooms, finely sliced	4 oz
3	squab	3
150 mL	Marsala	5 fl oz
150 mL	water	5 fl oz
60 mL	olive oil	4 tbsp

2	medium onions, finely chopped	2
200 g	mushrooms, finely sliced	7 oz
50 g	wild rice	2 oz
300 g	brown rice	10 oz
15 mL	dried Japanese Hijiki seaweed (if you cannot get this, leave it out)	1 tbsp
300 mL	dry white wine	½ pint
600 mL	water	1 pint
	several sprigs of fresh coriander	

Put the onions or shallots with the mushrooms, squab, Marsala and water in a pan just big enough to hold them. Season them lightly, cover them, bring to the boil and simmer gently for 1 hour. Remove the pigeons and strain the juices, reserving both vegetables and cooking liquid.

Take the flesh from the squab, pull it into bite-sized pieces and discard the bones. Mix the flesh with the reserved vegetables.

Heat the oil in a heavy pan and gently fry the onions until they are just soft. Add the mushrooms and continue to cook for a further few minutes. Add the wild rice, brown rice and Hijiki, stir well together, then add the reserved cooking juices. Cook all together for a few minutes, then add the white wine and half of the water. Bring to the boil and continue to cook gently for approximately 20 minutes or until the rice is cooked. Add more water if the rice dries up. Season to taste.

To serve, pile the rice around the outside of a serving dish. Reheat the squab and vegetables in a microwave or over hot water and pile it in the middle of the rice. Sprinkle with the chopped coriander and serve at once.

PER SERVING	
Energy Kcals	615.32
Protein g	33.4
Fat g	25.18
Saturated fatty acids g	2.36
Monounsaturated fatty acids g	8.38
Polyunsaturated fatty acids g	1.9
Carbohydrate g	52.79
Total Sugars g	4.87
Sodium mg	119.58
Fibre g	2.36

Vegetables and Vegetarian Dishes

Baked Potatoes with Tomato and Cheese

Leek, Cucumber and Gruyère Flan

Peanut Butter Bean Pot

Quinoa and Cashew Nut Pilaf

Risotto with Red Peppers

Potato, Leek and Apple Pie

Sweet Potato and Tomato Bake

Mushroom and Sunflower Seed Flan

Mexican Rice with Pepper and Corn

Broccoli and Cauliflower au Gratin with Lima Beans

Broccoli and Tofu Stir Fry

Cranberry and Tofu Risotto

Stuffed Peppers

Slow Roast Vegetables with Artichokes

Green Pie for St. Patrick's Day

Beet and Egg Bake

Spinach and Artichoke Flan

Buckwheat Pancakes with Mushroom Sauce

Winter Vegetable Casserole

Carrots Braised with Lima Beans

Beets with Red Cabbage

Okra and Sweet Potato Bake

A Salad of Zucchini and Lima Beans

"Dressed" Parsnips

Stir Fried Sprouts with Ginger

Pizza Base and Tomato Sauce

Vegetable Dahl

Roman Cabbage

Ful Mesdames

Lima Bean Bourguignon

Baked Polenta

Since children often prefer baked potatoes with soft skins while adults like them with crisp skins, starting them in the microwave and then crisping up the skins for those who want them, in the oven, is an excellent way to keep everyone happy.

Baked Potatoes with Tomato and Cheese

Per person

A very simple way of "improving" a baked potato - if that is possible!

1 large or 2 small baking potatoes		
1	large tomato, sliced	1
50 g	strong Cheddar cheese, grated	2 oz
	freshly ground black pepper	

Bake the potatoes in the oven or in a microwave until they are cooked through. Take them out of the oven, split them lengthways and open them up. Put them on or in an ovenproof dish. Lay the slices of tomato, layered with the grated cheese over the open middle of the potato, leaving a layer of cheese on the top. Return the potatoes to a moderately hot oven (180°C/ 350°F) for about 20 minutes to crisp the outside of the skin, cook the tomatoes and melt the cheese. Grind over some black pepper and eat at once.

PER SERVING	
Energy Kcals	368.75
Protein g	17.58
Fat g	17.86
Saturated fatty acids g	12.93
Monounsaturated fatty acids g	6.78
Polyunsaturated fatty acids g	1.05
Carbohydrate g	36.78
Total Sugars g	3.58
Sodium mg	356.19
Fibre g	3.35

If you cannot find fresh chillies you can always use dried ones, soaked for 5 minutes in boiling water. Always be careful when dealing with chillies either to wear gloves or to wash your hands very well before touching your face or eyes as the chilli oil will burn.

Leek, Cucumber and Gruyère Flan

Serves 6

A rather unusual flan in which the crispness of the water chestnuts sets off the softness of the leeks and pineapple.

200 g	chick pea (gram) flour, sifted	7 oz
100 g	butter or low-fat spread	4 oz
30 mL	sunflower oil	2 tbsp
200 g	leeks, trimmed and sliced	7 oz
2	fresh red chilli peppers, trimmed and sliced	2
1/2	medium-sized cucumber, diced	1/2
100 g	tinned water chestnuts, drained	4 oz
100 g	tinned pineapple chunks, drained	4 oz
100 g	Gruyère or Emmenthal cheese	4 oz
	salt and pepper	

Heat the oven to 180°C/350°F.

Rub the butter or spread into the chick pea flour until it is light and crumbly, then add approximately 60 mL / 4 tablespoons of water to make it into a soft dough. Roll out the pastry and line a 20 cm/ 8 inch flan dish. Line it with foil, weight it down with baking beans and bake it blind.

Meanwhile, heat the oil in a flattish pan and gently cook the leeks and chilli for 5 minutes or until they are beginning to soften. Add the cucumber, cover the pan and sweat the vegetables for 10 minutes, then add the drained water chestnuts and pineapple chunks.

Spoon this mixture into the flan case, then lay the slices of cheese over the top.

Bake the flan for a further 15 minutes just to melt and brown the cheese.

Remove from the oven and grind over some black pepper. Serve warm or cold.

PER SERVING	
Energy Kcals	363.22
Protein g	11.83
Fat g	26.67
Saturated fatty acids g	13.77
Monounsaturated fatty acids g	6.94
Polyunsaturated fatty acids g	5.17
Carbohydrate g	21.27
Total Sugars g	4.69
Sodium mg	253.08
Fibre g	4.48

If you cannot get fresh ginger root you can always use 5 mL/ 1 teaspoon of ground ginger. The flavour will not be quite the same, but nearly as good. But be sure that it gets well cooked as raw spices do not taste nice.

Peanut Butter Bean Pot

Serves 4

Like all bean pots it pays to make it the day before you want to eat it, to allow the flavours to mature.

225 g	dried navy beans	8 oz
30 mL	peanut or sunflower oil	2 tbsp
3	sticks celery , diced	3
2	medium onions, diced	2
2	medium carrots, sliced into rounds	2
1	medium red pepper, seeded and sliced	1
25 g	ginger root, peeled and sliced very thinly	1 oz
300 mL	red wine	½ pint
900 mL	water	1½ pints
5 mL	black peppercorns	1 tsp
75 g	crunchy peanut butter - but check the ingredient panel for starch included in some varieties	3 oz
	salt	
	a good shake of Tabasco	
	fresh parsley, chopped roughly	

Soak the beans over night, then discard the water. Alternatively, bring them to the boil in plenty of unsalted water, boil briskly for 10 - 15 minutes, then drain.

Heat the oil in a heavy pan and gently fry the celery, onion, carrots, pepper and ginger root for 10 - 15 minutes or until they have softened slightly.

Add the beans along with the wine, water and peppercorns. Bring the whole lot to the boil and simmer for approximately 1 hour or until the water is absorbed and the beans cooked. If it looks as though the bean pot is getting too dry, add more water. Once the beans are cooked, add the peanut butter, salt (never add it before the beans are cooked or they will go rock hard) and Tabasco to taste. You may find that once the peanut butter is in, you need to add a little more water to reduce the sauce. Serve the bean pot generously sprinkled with lots of chopped parsley.

PER SERVING	
Energy Kcals	453.99
Protein g	15.83
Fat g	22.21
Saturated fatty acids g	3.08
Monounsaturated fatty acids g	10.77
Polyunsaturated fatty acids g	9.45
Carbohydrate g	38.19
Total Sugars g	9.84
Sodium mg	177.84
Fibre g	13.21

If you cannot find quinoa for this recipe, use an unhusked brown rice or a red Camargue rice, if you can get it.

Quinoa and Cashew Nut Pilaf

Serves 8

Quinoa is a South American, gluten-free grain not dissimilar to rice. It has a delicious nutty taste and the crunchy texture of brown rice. You should find it in good delicatessens or health food stores.

60 mL	olive oil	4 tbsp
300 g	leeks, finely sliced	10½ oz
2	sticks celery, chopped	2
250 g	quinoa	9 oz
300 mL	water	½ pint
300 mL	dry white wine	½ pint
200 g	water chestnuts, drained	7 oz
100 g	broken cashew nuts	4 oz
50 g	sunflower seeds	2 oz
	juice of 2 fresh lemons	
	salt and pepper	
2	sprigs fresh mint	2

Heat the oil in a heavy pan and cook the leeks and celery until just soft. Add the quinoa and the liquid. Bring to the boil and cook gently for 15 minutes until the quinoa is soft and has absorbed the liquid - add more if necessary. Drain the water chestnuts and halve them, then add to the mixture.

Brown the nuts and sunflower seeds in a dry pan, then add them to the pilaf along with lemon juice, salt and pepper to taste. Just before serving stir in the fresh chopped mint. Serve warm or cold.

PER SERVING	
Energy Kcals	315.13
Protein g	8.87
Fat g	18.66
Saturated fatty acids g	3.03
Monounsaturated fatty acids g	10.44
Polyunsaturated fatty acids g	4.79
Carbohydrate g	24.40
Total Sugars g	4.86
Sodium mg	86.29
Fibre g	1.82

Rices differ enormously in texture and taste. Italian risotto rice is fat, white and soft when cooked, absorbing lots of water, quite different to a brown unhusked rice which is nutty and crunchy and absorbs relatively little liquid.

Risotto with Red Peppers

Serves 4

If you are feeling energetic, char the peppers under a broiler, run them under cold water and remove their skins. This gives the peppers an even sweeter and more delicious taste and texture but is fiddly and time consuming, so can be left out if you are short of time.

60 mL	olive oil	4 tbsp
2	cloves garlic, sliced	2
2	large red peppers, seeded and finely sliced	2
400 g	tinned tomatoes	14 oz
1	bay leaf	1
5	fresh basil leaves, or 5mL / 1 teaspoon dried basil	5
300 g	arborio Italian risotto rice	10½ oz
800 mL	hot vegetable stock	1½ pints
	salt and pepper	

Heat 30 mL / 2 tablespoons of the oil in a wide heavy pan. Add the garlic and peppers and cook gently for 5 - 10 minutes or until the peppers are quite soft, then add the tomatoes and the bay leaf and dried basil, if you are using dried.

Continue to cook gently for a further 15 minutes.

Add the rice and mix well. Add half the hot liquid, stir well and continue to cook. Stir every now and then to prevent the rice sticking and when the liquid is absorbed, continue to add more until the rice is quite cooked. Add the rest of the oil and salt and pepper to taste if needed. Cover and set aside for 10 minutes before serving. Stir in the chopped fresh basil, if you are using it, as you are about to serve.

PER SERVING	
Energy Kcals	455.43
Protein g	7.95
Fat g	15.91
Saturated fatty acids g	3.21
Monounsaturated fatty acids g	12.48
Carbohydrate g	69.79
Polyunsaturated fatty acids g	2.89
Total Sugars g	9.69
Sodium mg	237.69
Fibre g	2.40

Right:
Fruit Crumble
(page 160)

If you cannot find cooking apples, use a tart eating apple such as a Granny Smith and add a squeeze of lemon juice.

Potato, Leek and Apple Pie

Serves 6

The cooking apples give a refreshing sharpness to this dish.

1.5 kg	old potatoes, well scrubbed	3 lb 5 oz
60 mL	olive oil	4 tbsp
3	medium onions, peeled and roughly chopped	3
	small head of celery, chopped	
2	large cooking apples, peeled, cored and diced	2
30 mL	potato flour	2 tbsp
450 mL	milk	16 fl oz
75 g	hazelnuts	3 oz
	salt and pepper	
	sesame seeds	

Slice the potatoes quite thinly, then par-cook them in a steamer or microwave. They will take around 10 minutes depending on the type of potato. Lay half of them out in the bottom of a flat, ovenproof dish and reserve the rest.

Meanwhile, heat 45 mL / 3 tablespoons of the oil in a heavy pan and gently cook the onions, celery and apple until the onion and celery are soft but not brown. Add the potato flour, stir well, then gradually add the milk and continue to cook until the sauce thickens slightly.

Break up the hazelnuts in a food processor until they are approximately halved, then lightly brown them under a broiler or in a pan with no oil, shaking all the time. Add them to the celery mixture. Season to taste.

Spoon this mixture over the potatoes in the bottom of the pan, then cover with the remaining slices of potato, layered tightly on top of each other. Brush the top of the potatoes with the remaining tablespoon of oil and sprinkle over the sesame seeds.

Bake the dish in a moderate oven (180°C/350°F) for 20 - 30 minutes or until the dish is well heated through and the potatoes on top are lightly browned. Serve at once.

PER SERVING	
Energy Kcals	570.78
Protein g	12.71
Fat g	30.38
Saturated fatty acids g	9.53
Monounsaturated fatty acids g	23.49
Polyunsaturated fatty acids g	4.59
Carbohydrate g	65.77
Total Sugars g	15.54
Sodium mg	388.10
Fibre g	7.48

Left:
Cheese Scones
(page 166)

Sweet potatoes or yams are increasingly popular and are now to be found in many supermarkets as well as West Indian stores and markets.

Sweet Potato and Tomato Bake

Serves 6

This combination of vegetables is quite sweet, although really delicious, so serve it with a crisp green salad with a tart lemon dressing to redress the balance.

1 kg	sweet potato, peeled and sliced thinly	2 lb 4 oz
45 mL	sunflower oil	3 tbsp
1 kg	tomatoes	2 lb 4 oz
25 g	light brown sugar	1 oz
200 g	Cheddar cheese, grated	7 oz
300 mL	whipping cream or sour cream	10 fl oz
	salt and pepper	
2	small packages plain potato chips (gluten free), crushed with a rolling pin	2

Heat 30 mL / 2 tablespoons of the oil in a heavy pan and briskly fry the sweet potato slices on both sides until they are lightly browned. Grease a casserole dish with the rest of the oil. Layer the sweet potato slices and the tomatoes alternately, sprinkling each layer lightly with salt, pepper, sugar, cheese and cream and ending with a layer of sweet potato topped with cream and cheese. Sprinkle the chips over the top and bake in a moderately hot oven (160°C / 325°F) for 40 - 50 minutes or until the sweet potato is cooked and the top browned.

PER SERVING	
Energy Kcals	642.03
Protein g	13.07
Fat g	44.6
Saturated fatty acids g	23.93
Monounsaturated fatty acids g	13.94
Polyunsaturated fatty acids	5.66
Carbohydrate g	50.51
Total Sugars g	20.46
Sodium mg	477.79
Fibre g	6.08

When using frozen spinach always remember to drain it very thoroughly, pressing the water out with the back of a wooden spoon. It retains a great deal of water which can spoil a dish like this flan.

Mushroom and Sunflower Seed Flan

Serves 4

A lovely flan for a summer lunch, it can be prepared in advance and tastes as good cold as warm.

75 g	chick pea (gram) flour	3 oz
75 g	rice flour	3 oz
75 g	butter or low-fat spread	3 oz
45 mL	walnut or sunflower oil	3 tbsp
150 g	fresh baby corn, whole or halved as you prefer	5 oz
50 g	sunflower seeds	2 oz
200 g	button mushrooms, wiped, whole if they are small, otherwise halved	7 oz
75 g	fresh spinach or defrosted frozen leaf spinach	3 oz
	juice of 1 lemon	
	salt and freshly ground black pepper	

Heat the oven to 180°C/350°F.

Make the pastry by rubbing the butter or spread into the flour then adding enough water to make a firm dough. Roll it out and line a 23 - 25 cm / 8 - 9 inch pie dish. Prick the bottom, line it with foil, weight it with beans or rice. Bake it for 10 minutes with the foil in, then 10 minutes without to get it nice and crisp.

Meanwhile, heat the oil in a heavy pan and add the corn and sunflower seeds. Fry briskly until they are lightly browned all over. Add the mushrooms, reduce the heat slightly and continue to cook for a couple of minutes. Then add the chopped spinach, stir well, cover the pan and cook for a further couple of minutes. Remove the lid, add the lemon juice and season well. Make sure the ingredients are well amalgamated, then spoon them into the flan case. Serve at once, warm, or leave to cool and serve at room temperature.

PER SERVING	
Energy Kcals	460.50
Protein g	10.04
Fat g	34.37
Saturated fatty acids g	12.02
Monounsaturated fatty acids g	7.67
Polyunsaturated fatty acids g	13.13
Carbohydrate g	28.58
Total Sugars g	2.22
Sodium mg	394.86
Fibre g	4.84

Tinned peppers are a useful standby to keep in the cupboard. They do not have the crunch of fresh peppers but are very flavoursome and colourful if you are using them in a cooked dish.

Mexican Rice with Pepper and Corn

Serves 6

This is a really pretty dish with the peppers and corn contrasting delightfully with the white rice.

45 mL	sunflower oil	3 tbsp
2	medium onions, peeled and finely chopped	2
1	small green pepper, seeded and finely sliced	1
1	small red pepper, seeded and finely sliced	1
1	small yellow pepper, seeded and finely sliced	1
1	red chilli pepper, seeded and finely sliced	1
300 g	white basmati rice	10 oz
600 mL	water or home-made vegetable stock	1 pint
100 g	tinned corn niblets, drained	4 oz
150 mL	plain yogurt, gluten free	5 fl oz
50 g	Cheddar cheese, grated	2 oz
	salt	
	Tabasco	

Heat the oil in a heavy pan and gently cook the onions, peppers and chilli until they are beginning to soften.

Add the rice, stir for a minute or two, then gradually add the stock. Bring to the boil and cook briskly until the liquid is absorbed and the rice is cooked. If necessary, add a little more stock.

Add the corn, yogurt and cheese and stir in well.

Season to taste with the sea salt and, if you want it to taste hotter, add Tabasco to taste. Serve just warm or at room temperature.

If the dish is too stiff, add a little more vegetable stock.

PER SERVING	
Energy Kcals	338.58
Protein g	8.84
Fat g	11.42
Saturated fatty acids g	3.44
Monounsaturated fatty acids g	3.33
Polyunsaturated fatty acids g	5.39
Carbohydrate g	50.17
Total Sugars g	7.01
Sodium mg	114.91
Fibre g	1.65

If you cannot get fresh cauliflower or broccoli for any dish you can use frozen but add them only at the end of the cooking process and make sure not to do more than heat them through or they will become very soggy.

Broccoli and Cauliflower au Gratin with Lima Beans

Serves 6

Cauliflower cheese is always a popular dish so it seems worth using it as a basis for other variations on the same theme.

1	large onion, peeled and chopped	1
300 g	cauliflower florets	10 oz
500 g	broccoli florets	1 lb 2 oz
50 g	butter	2 oz
50 g	potato flour	2 oz
15 mL	wholegrain mustard	1 tbsp
600 mL	milk	1 pint
150 g	Cheddar cheese, grated	5 oz
2 tbsp	fresh Parmesan, grated	2 tbsp
1	tin (400 g) lima beans, drained	1
25 g	flaked almonds	1 oz
1	small package ordinary potato chips, gluten free, crushed	1
	salt and pepper	

Steam or microwave the onion, cauliflower and broccoli florets until they are just cooked but still slightly *al dente*. Set aside.

Meanwhile, melt the butter in the pan and add the potato flour to make a roux. Add the mustard, then gradually add the milk, stirring continuously until you get a smooth sauce. Add two thirds of the cheeses and stir until they are melted. Season to taste, remembering that the chips on the top will probably already be salted.

Carefully add the vegetables, the lima beans and the almonds and, mixing gently, gradually bring the dish back to just below boiling point.

To serve, spoon the mixture into a heatproof casserole dish, mix the remaining cheese with the chips, sprinkle them over the top of the dish and pass under the broiler to brown lightly.

PER SERVING	
Energy Kcals	425.22
Protein g	22.58
Fat g	27.18
Saturated fatty acids g	14.86
Monounsaturated fatty acids g	8.73
Polyunsaturated fatty acids g	2.60
Carbohydrate g	24.11
Total Sugars g	9.85
Sodium mg	632.98
Fibre g	6.44

If you do not have a wok you can still stir fry quite successfully in a deep, wide frying pan - just make sure that your oil is very hot and that you work quickly.

Broccoli and Tofu Stir Fry

Serves 4

Broccoli is always wonderful in a stir fry as it keeps its colour so well. Do not be tempted to season with soy sauce unless you are sure it is a wheat- and gluten-free brand.

60 mL	sunflower or stir fry oil	4 tbsp
25 g	fresh ginger root, peeled and very finely sliced	1 oz
2	large cloves garlic, finely sliced	2
1	small green chilli, seeded and very finely sliced	1
100 g	Jerusalem artichokes, well scrubbed and finely sliced in rounds	4 oz
400 g	broccoli, the stem sliced thinly and the heads broken into small florets	14 oz
200 g	marinated tofu, gluten free, diced	7 oz
50 g	sesame seeds	2 oz
	gluten-free soya sauce	

You may be able to buy ready marinated tofu in health food stores although you should check its ingredients. If you cannot get it, use a normal tofu but marinate in 15 mL /1 tablespoon of gluten-free soya sauce and 15 mL /1 tablespoon of lemon juice for an hour before using it.

Heat the oil in a wok and briskly fry the ginger, garlic and chilli. Do not allow them to burn.

Add the broccoli stems and finely sliced artichoke to the vegetables in the wok and continue to cook for a further few minutes.

Add the broccoli florets, tofu and sesame seeds and continue to cook briskly for a further 3 - 4 minutes or until the florets are just beginning to soften.

Serve at once, seasoned with gluten-free soya sauce to taste.

PER SERVING	
Energy Kcals	295.50
Protein g	11.72
Fat g	25.32
Saturated fatty acids g	3.55
Monounsaturated fatty acids g	6.58
Polyunsaturated fatty acids g	14.45
Carbohydrate g	5.93
Total Sugars g	2.29
Sodium mg	42.74
Fibre g	4.62

Most people only think of using cranberries at Christmas but they are a delicious, tart fruit to use at any time of the year, and you can always use frozen berries if you can't get fresh ones.

Cranberry and Tofu Risotto

Serves 4

A brightly coloured risotto. The cranberries and red pepper contrast strikingly with the rice while the crunch of the water chestnuts contrasts equally well with the softness of the fruit.

30 mL	olive oil	2 tbsp
2	medium leeks, finely sliced	2
1	medium sized red pepper, seeded and finely sliced	1
150 g	risotto rice	5 oz
100 g	fresh cranberries	4 oz
1	large, sharp eating apple, peeled, cored and diced	1
300 mL	dry white wine	½ pint
600 mL	water	1 pint
250 g	smoked or marinated tofu, gluten free, diced	9 oz
200 g	tinned water chestnuts, drained and halved	7 oz
	salt and pepper	

Heat the oil in a heavy pan, then gently cook the leeks and pepper until soft.

Add the rice, cranberries and apple, then the wine and water, stirring gently. Bring to a simmer and cook gently for 10 -15 minutes or until the rice is soft and the liquid absorbed. Add a little more liquid if necessary.

Add the tofu and the water chestnuts. Mix well and season to taste with salt and pepper. Serve warm or cold.

PER SERVING	
Energy Kcals	352.05
Protein g	9.65
Fat g	11.21
Saturated fatty acids g	2.06
Monounsaturated fatty acids g	7.10
Polyunsaturated fatty acids g	2.90
Carbohydrate g	42.79
Total Sugars g	10.61
Sodium mg	208.94
Fibre g	2.74

You can always make the stuffing for any stuffed pepper dish in advance and freeze it, merely defrosting it at room temperature for a couple of hours before you serve it.

Stuffed Peppers

Serves 6

A good dish for a buffet as they can be cooked in advance and are easy to eat with a fork - or even, at a push, fingers!

30 mL	olive oil	2 tbsp
1	large onion, roughly chopped	1
3	large cloves garlic, peeled and finely chopped	3
3	fresh red chillies, seeded and finely chopped	3
1	large red pepper	1
240 g	green lentils	9 oz
1 L	water	1¾ pints
	salt and freshly ground black pepper	
60 g	pitted black olives	2 oz
15 mL	sunflower seeds	1 tbsp
3	large yellow peppers, halved and with the seeds and ribs removed	3
	large bunch fresh parsley, chopped	

Heat the oil in a large pan and cook the onion, garlic, chillies and red pepper until they are all softening and lightly browned but not burned. Add the lentils, stir for a couple of minutes, then add the water. Bring to the boil and simmer for 20 - 30 minutes or until the lentils are cooked without being totally mushy. You may need to add more liquid as they cook. Add the olives and sunflower seeds, mix them in well then season to taste with salt and pepper. Pile the mixture into the pepper shells - if you have too much pile it around the outside of the shells - and, depending on how crisp you like your pepper shells, put them in a moderately hot oven (190°C / 375°F), covered, for 10 - 30 minutes. Sprinkle them lavishly with the chopped parsley just before serving. The peppers are good both hot and cold.

PER SERVING	
Energy Kcals	250.28
Protein g	12.97
Fat g	9.68
Saturated fatty acids g	2.4
Monounsaturated fatty acids g	6.22
Polyunsaturated fatty acids g	2.76
Carbohydrate g	29.93
Total Sugars g	8.97
Sodium mg	237.68
Fibre g	6.93

You can roast almost any combination of vegetables this way. A very easy and nutritious way to cook them.

Slow Roast Vegetables with Artichokes

Serves 4

A splendidly easy and quite delicious way to cook vegetables - to be eaten on their own or as an accompaniment to roast meat or a nut roast.

60 mL	olive oil	4 tbsp
4	turnips, peeled and sliced	4
4	leeks, sliced	4
1	medium red pepper, seeded and sliced	1
100 g	fresh spinach or frozen spinach leaf, defrosted	4 oz
2	tins (400 g) artichoke hearts, drained	2
2	tins (400 g) broad beans, drained	2
30 mL	pumpkin seeds	2 tbsp
15 mL	gluten-free soya sauce	1 tbsp
	black pepper	

Preheat the oven to 180°C / 350°F.

Put the oil in the bottom of an ovenproof casserole, then add all the other ingredients apart from the pumpkin seeds, gluten-free soya sauce and pepper. Cover the casserole. If you are in a hurry, cook the vegetables in a microwave on High for 4 minutes then transfer to the oven for 20 minutes. Alternatively, just cook them in the oven for 30 - 40 minutes or until the turnips are soft. Add the pumpkin seeds, mushroom ketchup and black pepper to taste.

Serve alone or with rice, baked potatoes or bread.

PER SERVING	
Energy Kcals	404.95
Protein g	20.81
Fat g	25.03
Saturated fatty acids g	6.01
Monounsaturated fatty acids g	16.24
Polyunsaturated fatty acids g	8.03
Carbohydrate g	26.86
Total Sugars g	10.78
Sodium mg	31.85
Fibre g	17.52

You could serve the flan with home-made wheat- and gluten-free bread (see page 189) coloured green with lots of fresh herbs!

Green Pie for St. Patrick's Day

Serves 6

This is a lovely flan for any day of the year but particularly good on March 17 when anyone with a speck of Irish blood wears green.

200 g	sifted chick pea (gram) flour	7 oz
100 g	butter	3½ oz
1	large, ripe avocado	1
50 g	pumpkin seeds	2 oz
25 g	shelled pistachio nuts	1 oz
100 g	fresh spinach	4 oz
5 mL	fresh marjoram or 2.5 mL/ ½ tsp dried	1 tsp
4	medium eggs	4
450 mL	milk	16 fl oz
	salt	
	black pepper	

Heat the oven to 160°C / 325°F.

Rub the butter into the gram flour until you have a sandy consistency. Add enough water to make a stiff paste and roll out. Line a 20 cm / 8 inch flan dish, prick with a fork then line it with foil and weight it with beans or rice to bake it blind - 10 minutes with the foil, then 10 minutes with the foil and beans or rice removed.

Peel and stone the avocado and chop its flesh into a reasonable size dice. Put the flesh in a large bowl with the pumpkin seeds and the pistachio nuts. Chop the spinach and add it along with the marjoram. In a separate bowl beat the eggs, add the milk and season well. Add the liquid mixture to green mixture, mix them together well and spoon into the flan case.

Bake in the oven for 35 minutes or until set and slightly risen. Serve warm or cold.

PER SERVING	
Energy Kcals	457.21
Protein g	17.75
Fat g	33.52
Saturated fatty acids g	14.08
Monounsaturated fatty acids g	11.34
Polyunsaturated fatty acids g	4.78
Carbohydrate g	23.08
Total Sugars g	5.75
Sodium mg	283.63
Fibre g	5.41

Beet and Egg Bake

Serves 4

A must for beet enthusiasts as it brings out not only the wonderful colour but the flavour of fresh beets.

300 g	beets, topped and tailed, scrubbed and diced	10 oz
300 g	turnips, topped and tailed, scrubbed and diced	10 oz
300 g	sharp eating apples, cored but not peeled, diced	10 oz
	sea salt	
	fresh ground black pepper	
4	large eggs	4
15 mL	sesame seeds	1 tbsp

Put the beets, turnips and apples in a large steamer and steam for approximately 20 minutes or until all are cooked. Purée in a food processor and season to taste with a little salt and pepper.

Spoon the mixture into a flattish ovenproof dish, smooth out and make 4 hollows. Break the eggs into the hollows and sprinkle over the sesame seeds.

Bake in a moderate oven (160°C/ 325°F) for 15 minutes or until the eggs are just set - they should not wobble when you shake the dish - and the topping is lightly browned. Serve at once.

PER SERVING	
Energy Kcals	200.58
Protein g	10.84
Fat g	10.49
Saturated fatty acids g	4.63
Polyunsaturated fatty acids g	3.29
Monounsaturated fatty acids g	6.43
Carbohydrate g	17.76
Total Sugars g	17.13
Sodium mg	341.86
Fibre g	4.84

It is worth keeping a stock of fresh seeds - pumpkin and sunflower in particular - in the cupboard as they make excellent snacks for wheat and gluten allergics and can be carried in a bag in your pocket or handbag.

Spinach and Artichoke Flan

Serves 6

Another excellent flan which can be prepared in advance and eaten warm or at room temperature.

100 g	chick pea (gram) flour	4 oz
50 g	butter	2 oz
150 g	ricotta cheese	5 oz
150 g	frozen leaf spinach, defrosted and drained	5 oz
150 g	artichoke hearts, tinned or frozen and drained or defrosted	5 oz
50 g	pumpkin seeds	2 oz
50 g	Gruyère cheese	2 oz
	pepper	

Heat the oven to 180°C / 350°F.

Rub the butter into the gram flour until you have a sandy consistency. Mix with a little water to make a soft dough. Roll out the pastry and line a 15 cm (6 inch) flan dish and bake blind - see Green Pie on page 124.

Spread the ricotta cheese over the bottom of the flan dish.

Mix the spinach with the pumpkin seeds and spread it over the ricotta cheese.

Arrange the artichoke hearts on the top then sprinkle liberally with the grated Gruyère. Return to the oven for a further 20 minutes.

Grind over some fresh black pepper as the flan comes out of the oven and serve hot or warm.

PER SERVING	
Energy Kcals	214.37
Protein g	8.82
Fat g	15.47
Saturated fatty acids g	7.79
Monounsaturated fatty acids g	4.12
Polyunsaturated fatty acids g	2.67
Carbohydrate g	10.82
Total Sugars g	1.61
Sodium mg	78.23
Fibre g	2.75

You might want to make a double batch of the pancake mixture as they are equally good with any other savoury filling and freeze well for future use.

Buckwheat Pancakes with Mushroom Sauce

Serves 4

Because the buckwheat flour is dark, both the pancakes and the mushroom filling are quite a dark, rich colour so serve them with a light, bright vegetable such as snow peas or a green salad with lots of yellow peppers.

100 g	buckwheat flour	3½ oz
1	large egg	1
100 mL	water	3½ fl oz
150 mL	milk	5 fl oz
30 mL	olive oil	2 tbsp
1	medium onion, peeled and finely chopped	1
1	clove garlic, finely chopped	1
200 g	button mushrooms, wiped and sliced	7 oz
25 g	potato flour	1 oz
300 mL	milk	10 fl oz
50 g	broken cashew nuts	2 oz
25 g	halved black olives	1 oz
	salt and pepper	
	fresh parsley, chopped	

To make the pancakes:

Whizz the buckwheat flour, egg, some salt, water and milk in a food processor, then allow batter to stand for 10 - 15 minutes.

Heat a pancake pan with a tiny dribble of oil. Pour one small ladleful of the mixture into the pan and cook quickly on both sides. The pancakes should be quite thin and you should get eight out of the mixture - four for the dish and four to fill with crab apple jelly or late autumn stewed plums for pudding! Set them aside with a layer of plastic wrap or greaseproof paper between each pancake.

To make the stuffing:

Heat the olive oil in shallow pan and cook the onion and garlic until just beginning to soften. Add the mushrooms and continue to cook briskly until the mushrooms are done and their juices running.

Add the potato flour off the heat, stir in well, then gradually, still

PER SERVING	
Energy Kcals	375.81
Protein g	12.27
Fat g	21.32
Saturated fatty acids g	5.90
Monounsaturated fatty acids g	11.94
Polyunsaturated fatty acids g	2.55
Carbohydrate g	36.40
Total Sugars g	8.14
Sodium mg	528.10
Fibre g	2.73

off the heat, add the milk and stir until the sauce is quite smooth. Return to the heat and continue to stir until the sauce thickens. Add the cashews and the olives and continue to cook for a couple of minutes to allow the flavours to amalgamate. Season lightly to taste with salt and pepper, then add the chopped parsley.

Arrange the pancakes either flat on a plate with a layer of the filling in between each pancake to make a "cake," or fill each pancake with the filling and fold them over. You can arrange them on one big plate or on four individual plates. Cover with plastic wrap and reheat for 2½ minutes each for the individual pancakes / about 6 minutes for the cake in a microwave on high. Alternatively, cover tightly with aluminum foil and reheat in a moderate oven for about 30 minutes before serving.

Like the oven baked vegetables, this is another dish where you can vary the vegetables according to what you have in your fridge, or your own personal favourites.

Winter Vegetable Casserole

Serves 8

A very easy dish to prepare and excellent either on its own or as an accompaniment to roast meat or a vegetarian roast.

300 g	old potatoes	10½ oz
300 g	parsnip	10½ oz
300 g	turnip	10½ oz
300 g	celeriac	10½ oz
200 g	celery	7 oz
200 g	fennel	7 oz
6	bay leaves	6
800 g	tinned tomatoes	1 lb 12 oz
100 mL	dry white wine	3½ floz
300 g	brussels sprouts	10½ oz
	large handful of fresh parsley	

Peel and cut the root vegetables into fairly large dice or pieces. Chop the fennel and celery. Put both lots of vegetables into a heavy, ovenproof casserole with the bay leaves, tinned tomatoes and white wine. Mix together well, cover and cook gently on the stove top or in a low oven (150°C/300°F) for up to an hour or until all the vegetables are virtually cooked. Stir every now and then to mix the vegetables around.

When the root vegetables are all but cooked, add the sprouts and continue to cook for 15 minutes until the sprouts are soft but not soggy.

Adjust the seasoning although I do not find that it needs any salt or pepper.

Just before serving, sprinkle large quantities of freshly chopped parsley over the vegetables.

PER SERVING	
Energy Kcals	117.71
Protein g	4.79
Fat g	1.81
Saturated fatty acids g	1.55
Monounsaturated fatty acids g	1.59
Polyunsaturated fatty acids g	.94
Carbohydrate g	19.74
Total Sugars g	10.01
Sodium mg	77.83
Fibre g	8.04

Use young but not miniature vegetables if you want them to have any flavour.

Carrots Braised with Lima Beans

Serves 6

If you want to turn this into a meat dish - very popular with children - add 210 g / 7½ oz frankfurters, sliced in thick rounds along with the lima beans and peas.

600 g	young carrots, sliced in moderately thick rounds	1 lb 5 oz
2	tins (400 g) lima beans, drained	2
400 g	frozen petits pois	14 oz
120 mL	fresh lemon juice	4 fl oz
90 mL	olive oil	6 tbsp
	salt and black pepper	

Steam the carrots in a large steamer for 15 - 20 minutes or until they are just cooked. Add the lima beans and peas and continue to steam for a further 5 minutes until all are well warmed through.

Remove from the steamer into a dish and dress with the salt, pepper, lemon juice and olive oil - you may need to adjust the seasoning to your own taste.

If you want to feed this dish to children, I suggest you omit the lemon juice and oil.

PER SERVING	
Energy Kcals	306.72
Protein g	12.52
Fat g	16.99
Saturated fatty acids g	2.67
Polyunsaturated fatty acids g	2.79
Monounsaturated fatty acids g	13.12
Carbohydrate g	28.19
Total Sugars g	9.46
Sodium mg	662.65
Fibre g	11.86

A combination of Brussels sprouts and red cabbage, finely sliced, also makes an excellent winter salad - especially mixed with cooked potato.

Beets with Red Cabbage

Serves 4

A wonderfully coloured dish with a very Russian feel to it.

200 g	small raw beets, scrubbed and halved or quartered if large	7 oz
250 g	Brussels sprouts, trimmed and halved if large	9 oz
200 g	red cabbage, sliced	7 oz
25 g	currants	1 oz
5 mL	caraway seeds	1 tsp
45 mL	red wine	3 tbsp
45 mL	water	3 tbsp
45 mL	plain low-fat yogurt, gluten free	3 tbsp
50 g	broken cashew nuts	2 oz
25 g	sesame seeds	1 oz
2.5 mL	potato flour	½ tsp
150 mL	milk	5 fl oz
250 mL	plain low fat yogurt, gluten free	9 fl oz
	juice of ½ - 1 lemon	
	salt and pepper	

Steam the beet quarters in a steamer for 5 minutes, then add the sprouts. Continue to cook for a further 10 - 15 minutes or until both are *al dente*. Cut the beets into medium-sized dice.

Meanwhile, put the red cabbage, currants and caraway seeds in a large heavy pan with the wine, water and yogurt. Cover and cook gently for 10 - 15 minutes or until the cabbage is also *al dente*.

Mix all the vegetables together, then add the cashews and sesame seeds. You can leave it at this point and serve the dish warm on its own or as a vegetable.

If you want to make the sauce, mix the potato flour with a little of the milk to make a smooth paste. Add the rest of the milk and heat slowly, stirring all the time, until the sauce thickens. Remove from the heat and add the yogurt and lemon juice, then season to taste. Reheat but do NOT boil or the sauce will curdle, and pour over the vegetables to serve.

PER SERVING	
Energy Kcals	264.41
Protein g	12.63
Fat g	13.07
Saturated fatty acids g	4.25
Monounsaturated fatty acids g	6.63
Polyunsaturated fatty acids g	4.19
Carbohydrate g	24.24
Total Sugars g	19.57
Sodium mg	324.37
Fibre g	5.93

Brightly coloured dishes like this are great to serve in winter as they make you feel as though there is sun around, even when there is not!

Okra and Sweet Potato Bake

Serves 4

Another brightly coloured vegetable casserole which works just as well as a dish on its own or as an accompaniment to any well-flavoured meat dish.

2	large green chillies, seeded and finely sliced	2
1	large clove garlic, finely sliced	1
150 g	okra, topped and tailed and sliced into rings	5½ oz
200 g	fresh or frozen leaf spinach	7 oz
400 g	tinned tomatoes	14 oz
100 mL	vegetable stock	3½ fl oz
150 g	green beans, topped and tailed and sliced across	5½ oz
	salt and pepper	
600 g	sweet potato, peeled and very thinly sliced	1 lb 5 oz
15 mL	olive oil	1 tbsp

Heat the oven to 180°C/350°F.

Put the chilli, garlic, okra, spinach and tomatoes in a heavy pan and bring gently to the boil. Simmer for 15 - 20 minutes, adding a little vegetable stock if the mixture seems too dry. Add the green beans and season to taste. Spoon the mixture into an ovenproof casserole.

Lay the potatoes out over the top, carefully overlapping each slice. Cover the casserole and cook in a moderate oven for 25 minutes or until the sweet potatoes are almost cooked.

Remove the lid, brush the top of the potatoes with the oil and return to the oven, uncovered, for a further 15 minutes to brown the top.

PER SERVING	
Energy Kcals	278.56
Protein g	9.63
Fat g	9.62
Saturated fatty acids g	1.88
Monounsaturated fatty acids g	5.59
Polyunsaturated fatty acids g	2.01
Carbohydrate g	41.23
Total Sugars g	14.71
Sodium mg	4567.46
Fibre g	7.90

As always with fresh coriander, if you cannot get it (try an Indian store if it is not in the supermarket), or if you do not like it, replace it with flat-leaved or ordinary fresh parsley.

A Salad of Zucchini and Lima Beans

Serves 6

A substantial salad to serve as a main course or, in smaller quantities, as a starter.

90 mL	olive oil	6 tbsp
6	medium zucchini, thickly sliced	6
300 g	marinated or smoked tofu, gluten free, in fairly large dice	10 oz
450 g	tinned lima beans, drained	1 lb
100 g	pitted black olives	4 oz
	salt and pepper	
	fresh coriander, roughly chopped	

Cook the zucchini briskly in the oil until they are all lightly browned but still *al dente*. Add the tofu, lima beans and olives (whole or halved as you prefer) and leave on a very low heat for 5 minutes to allow the flavours to amalgamate. Remove from the heat and season to taste with salt and pepper.

The salad can be served warm or at room temperature but in either case stir in the fresh, chopped coriander just before serving.

PER SERVING	
Energy Kcals	262.6
Protein g	10.45
Fat g	19.67
Saturated fatty acids g	2.79
Monounsaturated fatty acids g	13.39
Polyunsaturated fatty acids g	3.21
Carbohydrate g	11.89
Total Sugars g	2.66
Sodium mg	759.67
Fibre g	4.68

If you are a sweet potato fan you could also try this with sweet potatoes.

"Dressed" Parsnips

Serves 6

This is a seventeenth-century recipe and is quite the most delicious way of serving parsnips that I know.

1 kg	parsnips, scrubbed and sliced	2 lb 4 oz
1 L	milk	1¾ pints

Put the parsnips in a large pan with the milk and bring gently to the boil. Simmer for 45 minutes - 1 hour or until the parsnips are quite soft. Drain them, reserving the milk. Purée them in a food processor or blender then return them to the pan. Reheat them slowly, gradually stirring in all the milk that they were cooked in. You can add seasoning if you want but I do not find it is necessary. Serve them at once or set aside and reheat to serve when needed.

PER SERVING	
Energy Kcals	216.67
Protein g	8.33
Fat g	8.33
Saturated fatty acids g	4.33
Monounsaturated fatty acids g	2.67
Polyunsaturated fatty acids g	.50
Carbohydrate g	28.83
Total Sugars g	17.50
Sodium mg	108.33
Fibre g	7.67

If you want to keep the Chinese feel and make your family really work for their supper, get them to eat the sprouts with chopsticks!

Stir Fried Sprouts with Ginger

Serves 4

Most people think of sprouts only as a rather overcooked green vegetable with Christmas turkey but they have endless other possibilities as vegetables. Do not be tempted to use soy sauce unless you are absolutely sure that it does not contain wheat or gluten.

30 mL	sesame , stir fry or sunflower oil	2 tbsp
4	large cloves of garlic, peeled and very thinly sliced	4
40 g	fresh ginger root, peeled and very finely sliced	1½ oz
400 g	Brussels sprouts, trimmed and finely sliced	14 oz
75 g	broken cashew nuts	3 oz
	salt and pepper	

Heat the oil in a wok and lightly fry the garlic and ginger for 4 - 5 minutes, making sure they do not burn. Add the sprouts and cashew nuts and cook quite fast for 2 - 3 minutes or until the sprouts are just beginning to soften. Season with salt and pepper and serve at once.

PER SERVING	
Energy Kcals	225.01
Protein g	7.48
Fat g	18.01
Saturated fatty acids g	3.17
Monounsaturated fatty acids g	8.17
Polyunsaturated fatty acids g	5.67
Carbohydrate g	9.13
Total Sugars g	4.28
Sodium mg	81.66
Fibre g	4.91

The simplest pizza topping is a tomato sauce but you can ring the changes with additional toppings such as:
- grated cheese
- slices of Mozzarella
- olives
- capers
- sliced mushrooms
- diced peppers
- salami
- bacon
- ham
- corn niblets

Pizza Base and Tomato Sauce

Serves 4

Pizza is such a popular dish these days, especially with children, that it is hard to have to miss out on it. This recipe make a slightly bready but very acceptable pizza base.

150 g	chick pea (gram) flour	5 oz
2.5 mL	salt	1/2 tsp
1 mL	instant yeast granules, gluten free	1/4 tsp
15 mL (or less)	olive oil	scant tbsp
90 mL	(about) luke warm water	6 tbsp
400 g	tinned tomatoes	14 oz
1	large clove garlic, chopped	1
2.5 mL	dried basil	1/2 tsp
	pinch dried oregano	
	pinch dried parsley	
	salt	
	pepper	

Mix the flour, salt and yeast granules in a bowl. Make a well in the middle and add the oil then, gradually, stirring all the time with a fork, add the warm water. Continue to mix until you have a rough ball of dough. (If it is too sticky, add more flour; if there are dry patches of flour, add more water.) Once the dough has come together in a ball, take it out and knead it by pushing it flat with the ball of your hand, then folding it over into a new ball and flattening it all over again. You should continue to knead for 8 - 10 minutes by which time the dough should have become quite elastic.

Put the ball of dough into a clean bowl, cut a cross in the top with a knife, cover the bowl tightly with plastic and put in a warm, draft free place to rise. It should roughly double its size in 1 - 3 hours depending on the room temperature.

When the dough has risen, take it out of the bowl and knock the air out of the ball with your fist. On a floured board knead it again for a further few minutes, then flatten it with your hands. Roll the dough out with a rolling pin until it is no more than 2 cm (1 inch) thick in the middle - a little thicker at the edge - and place it on a flat baking tray.

Spread with tomato sauce (see below) and your chosen topping, then bake in a hot oven (220°C/400°F) for 8 - 12 minutes or until the topping and base are cooked. Serve at once.

PER PIZZA	
Energy Kcals	470.00
Protein g	22.00
Fat g	4.00
Saturated fatty acids g	0.40
Monounsaturated fatty acids g	0.90
Polyunsaturated fatty acids g	1.90
Carbohydrate g	85.00
Total Sugars g	33.00
Sodium mg	210.00
Fibre g	18.00

Tomato pizza topping
Put the tomatoes and garlic in a pan on a low heat and cook gently for 30 minutes. Add the herbs and continue to cook for a further 30 minutes until the tomatoes are well reduced. Season to taste.

Real Indian dahls are often quite liquid and are used more as a sauce than a dish on their own.

Vegetable Dahl

Serves 4

Dahl always seems to bring out the best in lentils. This makes an excellent quick supper dish.

30 mL	sunflower oil	2 tbsp
2	medium onions, finely sliced	2
1	large clove garlic, finely chopped	1
2.5 mL	ground cumin	1/2 tsp
1 mL	cayenne pepper	1/4 tsp
400 g	eggplant, diced	14 oz
100 g	red lentils	4 oz
600 mL	water or home-made vegetable stock	1 pint
	salt	
5 mL	tomato purée	1 tsp
225 g	potatoes, scrubbed and diced	8 oz
225 g	cauliflower florets	8 oz
5 mL	ground turmeric	1 tsp
10 mL	garam masala	2 tsp

Heat the oil in a heavy pan and gently fry the onions, garlic, cumin and cayenne for a couple of minutes. Add the eggplant, lentils, stock, salt and tomato purée, cover and simmer for approximately 30 minutes.

Meanwhile put the potatoes and cauliflower in two separate pans with a bare 2 cm / 1 inch water in the bottom to each of which you have added 2.5 mL / 1/2 teaspoon of turmeric. Cover them both and simmer until the vegetables are just tender, then drain.

When the eggplant mixture is ready, stir in the garam masala to taste and the drained vegetables. Serve with rice and popadoms.

PER SERVING	
Energy Kcals	251.28
Protein g	11.4
Fat g	9.21
Saturated fatty acids g	2.3
Monounsaturated fatty acids g	3.81
Polyunsaturated fatty acids g	5.51
Carbohydrate g	33.13
Total Sugars g	7.81
Sodium mg	83.78
Fibre g	5.91

Not only did the Romans believe that cabbage would cure hangovers but that lettuce would send you to sleep!

Roman Cabbage

Serves 4

This recipe is based on a Roman recipe which used cracked wheat instead of rice.

100 g	brown rice	4 oz
15 g	butter	½ oz
1	medium onion, finely sliced	1
450 g	savoy cabbage, chopped	1 lb
150 mL	water or home-made vegetable stock	5 fl oz
	salt and pepper	
50 g	pine nuts	2 oz
50 g	raisins	2 oz
10	coriander seeds	10
25 g	butter	1 oz

Cook the rice in plenty of fast boiling water or vegetable stock until it is just *al dente*.

Meanwhile, cook the finely sliced onion gently in the butter until it is transparent. Add the cabbage, mix the onion in well, then add the stock and a little seasoning. Cover the pan and simmer gently for approximately 15 minutes or until the cabbage is cooked but still slightly crunchy; it can also be cooked in a microwave for approximately 5 minutes on High.

Turn the cabbage into an ovenproof dish. Stir the pine nuts, raisins and coriander seeds into the rice and season lightly if needed. Spread the mixture over the cabbage in the dish and dot the top with butter. Cover and cook in a moderate oven (180°C / 350°F) for 20 minutes to allow the flavours to amalgamate before serving.

PER SERVING	
Energy Kcals	322.33
Protein g	6.45
Fat g	18.12
Saturated fatty acids g	6.51
Monounsaturated fatty acids g	6.02
Polyunsaturated fatty acids g	6.01
Carbohydrate g	35.95
Total Sugars g	15.25
Sodium mg	138.53
Fibre g	4.80

If you cannot get fava beans you can still use the same cooking on other dried beans - the taste will not be as authentic but it will still be good.

Ful Mesdames

Serves 6

Slowly cooked brown fava beans or ful is the national dish of Egypt. The beans are eaten by rich and poor, for breakfast, lunch and dinner, with bread, lentils, sauces, salads and slow-cooked eggs. Seasoning, apart from the addition of some garlic once the beans are cooked, is done at the table.

If you cannot get the proper ful use any dried broad bean, as ful come from the broad bean family.

750 g	dried ful or brown fava beans - they are obtainable in most Greek or Middle Eastern stores	1 lb 10 oz
4	large cloves garlic, finely chopped	4
	large bunch of fresh parsley	

Soak the rinsed beans for a minimum of 8 hours. Then put them in a large saucepan well covered with fresh water, bring to the boil, cover and simmer until they are tender but not mushy. This can take anything from 2 - 6 hours depending on how dry the beans were; if you have a slow cooker it can be used to cook the beans overnight. You can also cook them in a pressure cooker which reduces the cooking time to 30 - 45 minutes but remember that a microwave will not reduce the cooking time. When the beans are cooked, drain them and add the garlic.

Serve the beans warm, in bowls sprinkled with chopped parsley. Accompany them with oil or butter and lemon juice, salt, pepper, cumin and cayenne pepper.

PER SERVING	
Energy Kcals	368.6
Protein g	24.39
Fat g	2.25
Saturated fatty acids g	.50
Monounsaturated fatty acids g	.16
Polyunsaturated fatty acids g	1.01
Carbohydrate g	66.89
Total Sugars g	4.75
Sodium mg	52.88
Fibre g	20.55

If you cannot get button onions, use pickling onions or, if they drive you mad to peel, just use the smallest onions you can find and halve them.

Lima Bean Bourguignon

Serves 6

An excellent vegetarian version of Boeuf Bourguignon.

30 mL	sunflower oil	2 tbsp
2	cloves garlic, crushed	2
250 g	button onions, peeled but left whole	9 oz
2	small sticks celery, chopped	2
1	small red pepper, deseeded and sliced	1
200 g	button mushrooms, wiped and left whole	7 oz
5 mL	dried thyme	1 tsp
	small bunch fresh parsley, chopped	
2	bay leaves, fresh or dried	2
10	black peppercorns	10
25 g	potato flour	1 oz
300 mL	red wine	10 fl oz
300 mL	water or home-made vegetable stock	10 fl oz
400 g	lima beans, canned and drained	14 oz
400 g	flageolet beans*, canned and drained	14 oz
400 g	cannelini beans*, canned and drained	14 oz

Heat the oil in a heavy-based pan and gently cook the garlic, onions, celery and pepper until soft but not brown.

Add the mushrooms, herbs and peppercorns. Continue to cook for another few minutes, then add the potato flour. Make sure it is well amalgamated, then add the red wine and the stock and season lightly. Bring back to the boil and simmer gently for 30 minutes.

Add the beans and gradually bring back to the boil and simmer until the beans are well heated through. Adjust seasoning to taste before serving.

* If you cannot find these products, use red kidney beans and white kidney beans respectively.

PER SERVING	
Energy Kcals	317.39
Protein g	16.94
Fat g	6.72
Saturated fatty acids g	1.51
Monounsaturated fatty acids g	4.68
Polyunsaturated fatty acids g	3.9
Carbohydrate g	41.67
Total Sugars g	6.63
Sodium mg	1070.77
Fibre g	13.27

Baked Polenta

Serves 6

A favourite north Italian dish. This recipe is based on one in Anna del Conte's wonderful book, *The Classic Food of Northern Italy*. You can make the polenta the day before you need it, then combine it with the sauce when you need to cook the dish.

200 g	coarse polenta	7 oz
1 L	water	1¾ pints
45 mL	olive oil	3 tbsp
3	whole cloves garlic, peeled but left whole	3
400 g	mixed mushrooms of your choice, roughly chopped	14 oz
6	leaves fresh basil, chopped	6
25 g	butter	1 oz
20 g	cornstarch	1 oz
300 mL	whole milk	10 fl oz
100 mL	medium sherry	4 fl oz
100 g	mozzarella	4 oz
200 g	Gorgonzola	7 oz
100 g	Parmesan	4 oz
	sea salt	

Heat the oven to 180°C / 350°F.

Bring the water to a simmer with the salt. Gradually add the polenta to the water (Italians would let it run through their fingers) stirring all the time. Bring back to the simmer and cook, stirring all the time, for 5 minutes. Oil a shallow ovenproof dish and spoon in the polenta mix. Cover with oiled foil and bake for 1 hour.

Take out of the oven and, with the foil still on top, leave to get quite cold.

To make the bake, reheat the oven.

Heat the oil in a heavy pan and add the garlic cloves, mushrooms and basil. Cook briskly for 5 - 8 minutes or until the mushrooms are cooked through.

Meanwhile, melt the butter in a small pan, add the cornstarch, mix well, then gradually add the milk, stirring all the time until the sauce thickens. Add the sherry.

PER SERVING	
Energy Kcals	540.22
Protein g	23.57
Fat g	34.41
Saturated fatty acids g	17.07
Polyunsaturated fatty acids g	1.97
Monounsaturated fatty acids g	12.56
Carbohydrate g	31.33
Total Sugars g	3.92
Sodium mg	970.15
Fibre g	.84

Use a couple of tablespoons of the sauce to cover the bottom of a wide ovenproof casserole.

Turn the polenta out onto a board and cut half of it into medium thick (10mm/ ¼ inch) slices and lay a layer over the bechamel sauce. Spoon the mushrooms over the polenta, then cover it with slices of the mozzarella and Gorgonzola. Cut the remains of the polenta into more slices with which to cover the cheese.

Finally, cover the top layer of polenta with the rest of the sauce and sprinkle over the grated Parmesan.

Return to the oven and bake for a further 30 minutes to melt and amalgamate the cheese and sauces. Serve at once with a green salad.

Desserts

Carrot and Ginger Tart

Tipsy Hedgehog Cake

Cheesecake Pancakes

Pancakes

Hot Chocolate Soufflé

Fresh Fruit Sponge Gateau

Chocolate Roulade

Apple and Vermicelli Pudding

Crêpes Suzettes

Trifle

Bakewell Tart

Lemon Meringue Pie

Bread and Butter Pudding

Steamed Marmalade Pudding

Cranberry Rice Pudding

Lemon Cheesecake

Fruit Crumbles

Rhubarb Crumble

Baked Fruit Flan

Sweet Rum Omelette

Upside Down Ginger and Pear Pudding

Natural fruit sweeteners like puréed carrots, apples or pears give a delicious flavoursome sweetness, quite unlike - and much nicer than - the pure sweetness of white sugar.

Carrot and Ginger Tart

Serves 4

A rather unusual, but delicious, tart which uses the natural sweetness of carrots to contrast with the spiciness of the ginger.

50 g	sieved chick pea (gram) flour	2 oz
50 g	rice flour	2 oz
75 g	butter	3 oz
50 g	broken walnuts	2 oz
300 g	young carrots, scrubbed and sliced thickly	10 oz
60 mL	ginger wine	4 tbsp
60 mL	apple juice	4 tbsp
2	eggs	2
50 g	crystallized or stem ginger rinsed free of syrup/sugar	2 oz

Mix the flours together and rub in the butter. When it is well crumbled, add the walnuts and enough water to make a firm paste. Roll this out and line an 18 cm / 7 inch flan case; reserve the pastry scraps. Line the flan case with foil, weight it with beans and bake it in a moderate oven (180°C /350°F) for 10 minutes. Remove the beans and foil and cook for a further 5 minutes or until the pastry is cooked through, then take it out of the oven and set it aside.

Meanwhile put the carrots in a heavy pan with the ginger wine and apple juice, cover it tightly and simmer it gently for 30 minutes by which time the carrots should be quite soft. Purée the carrots in a food processor with the 2 eggs.

Chop the preserved ginger into quite small pieces (how small will depend on what size bits you would like to find in your tart) and mix them into the carrot purée. Spoon this into the flan case and use the pastry scraps to decorate the top with latticework ribbons, pastry balls or decorate with finely grated carrot. Reduce the oven to 170°C / 325°F and return the tart for 20 minutes by which time the pastry decoration should be cooked and the filling set. Serve warm or cold with cream, yogurt or ice cream.

PER SERVING	
Energy Kcals	400.21
Protein g	9.69
Fat g	28.36
Saturated fatty acids g	12.07
Monounsaturated fatty acids g	7.72
Polyunsaturated fatty acids g	7.38
Carbohydrate g	24.88
Total Sugars g	8.01
Sodium mg	222.5
Fibre g	3.98

If you are making this for children to eat, substitute their favourite fruit juice for the sherry and brandy.

Tipsy Hedgehog Cake

Serves 10

This is a great dessert for a party as it looks so spectacular yet is very easy to make and can be prepared well in advance. If you prefer a lighter sponge use the rice flour sponge on page 180.

200 g	butter	7 oz
200 g	light brown sugar	7 oz
3	medium eggs	3
200 g	sifted gram/chick pea flour	7 oz
15 mL, hpd	wheat- and gluten-free baking powder	1 hpd tsp
5 mL	vanilla	1 tsp
300 mL	medium sweet sherry	10 fl oz
60 mL	brandy	4 tbsp
50 g	flaked almonds	2 oz
600 mL	custard or lightly whipped cream	1 pint

Beat the butter with the sugar until light and fluffy. Beating slowly, add the eggs alternately with the flour. Fold in any remaining flour, the baking powder and vanilla. Spoon into a well-oiled or lined 20 cm (8 inch) tin and bake in a moderate oven (180°C/ 350°F) for 30 minutes or until the cake is firm to the touch and a skewer comes out clean. Cool on a rack.

Arrange your cake on your serving dish and prick it thoroughly all over with a skewer. (If you want it to look really like a hedgehog, trim two sides into a head and a tail.)

Mix the brandy with the sherry and slowly pour it over the cake allowing it to soak in thoroughly - your cake should end up really soggy.

Stick the almonds all over the cake (if it is to be a hedgehog slant them all backwards then make it a nose and two eyes with some currants). Serve it accompanied by the custard or cream.

PER SERVING	
Energy Kcals	459.47
Protein g	10.89
Fat g	25.76
Saturated fatty acids g	13.55
Monounsaturated fatty acids g	8.01
Polyunsaturated fatty acids g	2.23
Carbohydrate g	38.76
Total Sugars g	29.11
Sodium mg	276.36
Fibre g	2.51

Cheesecake Pancakes

Serves 4

You can use these pancakes with any other sweet mixture that you fancy.

100 g	chick pea flour	4 oz
200 mL	water	7 fl oz
350 g	ricotta cheese	12 oz
75 g	plump raisins	3 oz
	juice of 1 lemon	
40 g	granulated sugar	1½ oz
	salt	

Mix the flour, salt and water in a food processor, then allow it to stand for 10 - 15 minutes. Heat a pancake pan with a tiny dribble of oil. Pour one small ladleful of the mixture into the pan and cook quickly on both sides, then stack them with a piece of plastic wrap between each pancake.

In a bowl mix the cheese with the raisins, lemon juice and sugar to taste. Divide the mixture in 8 and fill each pancake; fold it into a neat parcel and lay in a flameproof serving dish. Sprinkle them with the extra sugar and put them under a hot broiler to caramelize the sugar topping. Serve at once.

PER SERVING	
Energy Kcals	268.58
Protein g	11.41
Fat g	7.79
Saturated fatty acids g	4.13
Monounsaturated fatty acids g	2.26
Polyunsaturated fatty acids g	1.00
Carbohydrate g	41.12
Total Sugars g	29.37
Sodium mg	145.9
Fibre g	3.07

Right:
Top: Lemon Shortbread
(page 171);
Bottom: Aunt Vi's Ginger Cookies
(page 179)

Do involve children when you are making pancakes. Whether or not they actually make them they can still have great fun tossing them - and if you lose a few to the floor, the mixture is so cheap that it really does not matter.

Pancakes

Serves 4

These pancakes freeze well so it might be worth making a big batch then freezing them, interleaved with plastic wrap or greaseproof paper so that you can just peel off as many as you need.

100 g	chick pea (gram) flour	4 oz
	salt	
200 mL	water	7 fl oz
	juice of 2 lemons	
50 g	granulated sugar	2 oz
15 mL	sunflower oil	1 tbsp

Whizz the flour, salt and water in a food processor, then allow it to stand for 10 - 15 minutes. Heat a pancake pan with a tiny dribble of oil. Pour one small ladleful of the mixture into the pan and cook quickly on both sides.

The pancakes should be quite thick and you should get at least 8 out of the mixture.

If they are to be eaten at once, serve them from the pan with sugar and lemon juice.

If they are to be used for a later dish, stack them with a piece of plastic wrap between each pancake.

PER SERVING	
Energy Kcals	163.31
Protein g	5.18
Fat g	5.40
Saturated fatty acids g	.88
Monounsaturated fatty acids g	1.34
Polyunsaturated fatty acids g	3.35
Carbohydrate g	26.01
Total Sugars g	14.26
Sodium mg	107.84
Fibre g	2.71

Left:
Light Sponge
(page 180)

Soufflés are a great deal easier to make than everyone reckons - and very impressive. As long as you fold in plenty of well-whisked (but not over-whipped) egg whites you should be fine.

Hot Chocolate Soufflé

Serves 4

Although this is light it is seriously rich so serve it after a light meal - and have plenty of coffee ready!

5	egg whites	5
	small pinch salt	
200 g	caster sugar	7 oz
50 g	cocoa powder	2 oz
	a few drops vanilla	
whipping cream or Greek yogurt to serve with the soufflé		

Heat the oven to 180°C / 350°F and put in a pan of water (big enough to hold the soufflé dish) to allow the water to get warm. Lightly grease the soufflé dish.

Whisk the egg whites with the salt until pretty stiff. Whisk in 45 mL/ 3 tablespoons of the sugar, then fold in the rest with the cocoa powder and the vanilla. Spoon the mixture into the soufflé dish and cook in the pan of water for 30 - 40 minutes or until the soufflé is risen and crisp on top.

Serve at once with cream or Greek yogurt.

PER SERVING	
Energy Kcals	254
Protein g	7.31
Fat g	3.21
Saturated fatty acids g	2.10
Monounsaturated fatty acids g	1.40
Polyunsaturated fatty acids g	.58
Carbohydrate g	54.44
Total Sugars g	53.13
Sodium mg	240.53
Fibre g	1.51

If you want to be economical about this gateau, use slightly bruised fruit and put lots of it in the middle of the gateau with plenty of cream or ricotta cheese, then just sprinkle the top with icing sugar.

Fresh Fruit Sponge Gateau

Serves 10

This is a very flexible dessert which can be made with any fresh or tinned fruit of your choice.

1	light sponge cake, gluten free	1
200 g	ricotta cheese	7 oz
300 mL	whipping cream	10 fl oz
300 g	strawberries or other fresh seasonal fruit	10 oz

Make the sponge cake according to the recipe on page 180.

When it is cold, cut it in half horizontally and spread the lower half with the ricotta cheese.

Put a thin layer of fruit, sliced or halved if necessary, over the ricotta cheese and cover with the top of the cake.

Whisk the cream until it holds its shape and use it to cover the cake. Top the cream with the fresh fruit arranged in whatever pattern you choose.

PER SERVING	
Energy Kcals	420.39
Protein g	12.26
Fat g	20.87
Saturated fatty acids g	11.53
Monounsaturated fatty acids g	7.38
Polyunsaturated fatty acids g	1.60
Carbohydrate g	47.70
Total Sugars g	30.23
Sodium mg	104.74
Englyst fibre g	1.04

If you are using this for a party you can make it one, or even two days ahead but sprinkle it with icing sugar only when you are ready to use it.

Chocolate Roulade

Serves 8

A real 1960s favourite which has stood the test of time - and which has the advantage of containing no wheat or gluten!

175 g	plain chocolate	6 oz
5	eggs	5
175 g	granulated sugar	6 oz
45 mL	hot water	3 tbsp
25 g	icing sugar, gluten free	1 oz
300 mL	whipping cream	½ pint

Preheat the oven to 180°C / 350°F.

Line a Swiss roll tin with greaseproof paper and brush it well with oil.

Break the chocolate into a double boiler or basin over hot water and melt it slowly. Meanwhile separate the eggs and whisk the yolks with the sugar until lemon coloured. Remove the chocolate from the heat, stir in the hot water, then mix the chocolate with the egg yolk mixture. Whisk the whites until they hold their shape, then fold them into the chocolate mixture. Pour this into the Swiss roll tin, make sure it is evenly spread and bake it for 15 minutes or until it holds its shape when lightly pressed with the finger. Make sure the oven shelf is level or you will get a lopsided roll.

Once the roulade is cooked, take it out of the oven, cover it with a clean sheet of greaseproof paper and then with a wet tea towel - leave it for at least a couple of hours.

To finish the roulade, turn it onto a third piece of greaseproof paper, well dusted with icing sugar. Carefully peel off the lower sheet of paper - as long as you greased it well it should come off quite easily. Whisk the cream until it holds its shape, spread it over the roulade, then carefully roll it up with the lower sheet of paper and turn it onto a serving dish. Shake a little more icing sugar over the top. You can eat it immediately but it will be very squishy; alternatively chill it for a couple of hours to firm it up.

PER SERVING	
Energy Kcals	436.81
Protein g	6.60
Fat g	28.44
Saturated fatty acids g	16.11
Monounsaturated fatty acids g	9.01
Polyunsaturated fatty acids g	1.24
Carbohydrate g	41.81
Total Sugars g	40.62
Sodium mg	70.25
Fibre g	0.00

When dealing with rice noodles you need to cook them in fast-boiling water to keep them moving and separated, otherwise they have a habit of getting stuck together in a lump.

Apple and Vermicelli Pudding

Serves 4

Based on a Victorian apple dessert, this recipe is also very similar to the traditional Jewish Lockshen pudding.

2	large cooking apples	2
10 mL	ground cinnamon	2 tsp
25 g	light brown sugar	1 oz
	juice of ½ lemon	
200 mL	water	7 fl oz
50 g	golden raisins	2 oz
50 g	rice noodles	2 oz
2	eggs, separated	2

Heat the oven to 180°C / 350°F.

Core the apples, chop them and put them in a pan with the cinnamon, sugar, lemon juice and water. Bring to the boil and simmer for 5 - 8 minutes or until the apples are cooked. Purée them (complete with skins) in a food processor, then add the raisins.

Meanwhile cook the noodles in plenty of fast-boiling water for 4 minutes. Drain them and mix in the raisins and the apple. Separate the eggs and stir the yolks into the apple and noodle mixture. Lightly whisk the egg whites and fold them into the mixture.

Turn the pudding into an oiled deep pie dish and bake for 30 minutes by which time the pudding should be quite lightly risen, set and lightly browned on top. Serve warm, by itself or with cream or yogurt.

PER SERVING	
Energy Kcals	195.38
Protein g	5.16
Fat g	3.61
Saturated fatty acids g	2.89
Monounsaturated fatty acids g	3.37
Polyunsaturated fatty acids g	0.63
Carbohydrate g	37.61
Total Sugars g	27.43
Sodium mg	50.15
Fibre g	2.32

You can make all the elements of the crêpes in advance and freeze them individually, ready for final reheating and amalgamation when you are ready.

Crêpes Suzettes

Serves 6

A classic dish which works well with gram flour pancakes.

150 g	chick pea (gram) flour	5 oz
	salt	
250 mL	water	9 fl oz
50 mL	Cointreau or Grand Marnier	2 fl oz
75 g	granulated sugar plus 4 lumps of sugar	3 oz
	rind and juice of 2 oranges	
200 g	butter	7 oz
150 mL	Cointreau or Grand Marnier	5 fl oz
90 mL	brandy	6 tbsp

Mix the flour, salt and water in a food processor, then allow it to stand for 10 - 15 minutes. Rub the sugar lumps over the oranges until the sides of the lumps have absorbed all the oil from the orange skins. Remove the peel of the oranges with a vegetable peeler or very sharp knife, making sure that you do not get any pith. Mash the sugar lumps on a chopping board with the point of a heavy knife, then add the orange peel and the sugar and chop them all together until they are very finely minced. Scrape the mixture into a mixing bowl. Add the softened butter and beat until the mixture is light and fluffy - with an electric mixer if possible. Drop by drop add the orange juice and the orange liqueur - it must be done slowly or the butter will not absorb the liquid.

Heat a pancake pan with a tiny dribble of oil. Pour one small ladleful of the pancake batter into the pan and cook quickly on both sides. Stack the pancakes as you make them with a piece of plastic wrap between each pancake - you should get at least 12 out of the batter.

To serve:

Put the butter in a reasonably large chafing dish or heavy based frying pan and heat slowly until it is bubbling. Dip both sides of each crêpe in the butter until it is warm, fold it in half and then in half again to make a wedge and stack it at the side of the pan. Pour over the orange liqueur and stir into the butter sauce. Warm the brandy in a ladle or pan then pour it gently over the crêpes and light immediately, before it has time to amalgamate with the rest of the sauce. If you are nervous that it will not catch, cheat by lighting the brandy while it is still in the ladle and pour it over as it is flaming. Serve the crêpes at once.

PER SERVING	
Energy Kcals	552.22
Protein g	6.48
Fat g	28.65
Saturated fatty acids g	18.79
Monounsaturated fatty acids g	7.54
Polyunsaturated fatty acids g	2.21
Carbohydrate g	44.18
Total Sugars g	32.43
Sodium mg	330.82
Fibre g	3.81

If this is for children substitute their favourite fruit juices for the brandy and sherry.

Trifle

Serves 8

The gram flour makes quite a solid sponge which I think works well with trifle. If you prefer a lighter mixture, use the rice flour sponge on page 180.

100 g	butter	4 oz
100 g	light brown sugar	4 oz
1	large egg	1
100 g	sifted gram/chick pea flour	4 oz
5 mL, hpd	wheat- and gluten-free baking powder	1 hpd tsp
2	egg yolks	2
20 g	potato flour	3/4 oz
25 g	granulated sugar	1 oz
2.5 mL	vanilla	1/2 tsp
300 mL	milk	10 fl oz
45 mL	brandy	3 tbsp
100 mL	sweet sherry	3 1/2 fl oz
200 g	tinned peaches, drained of their juice	7 oz
100 mL	whipping cream	3 1/2 fl oz
2.5 mL	granulated sugar	1/2 tsp
5 mL	browned flaked almonds	1 tsp

Sponge:

Beat the butter with the sugar until light and fluffy. Beating slowly, add the egg with some of the flour. Fold in the remaining flour and baking powder. Spoon into a well oiled or lined 15cm / 6 inch baking tin (the shape does not matter) and bake in a moderate oven (180°C/350°F) for 20 minutes or until the cake is firm to the touch and a skewer comes out clean. Cool on a rack.

Custard:

In a small saucepan mix the egg yolks with the potato flour, sugar and vanilla then gradually add the milk. Heat slowly, stirring all the time until the custard thickens. Cool.

Do not tell anyone that you have made a wheat- and gluten-free Bread and Butter pudding. The custard will disguise the rather different texture of the bread so it will be fun to see if anyone notices.

Bread and Butter Pudding

Serves 6

Another great favourite usually barred to celiacs and wheat intolerants - but now gloriously resurrected!

4	slices of wheat- and gluten-free bread	4
25 g	butter	1 oz
25 g	currants	1 oz
25 g	raisins	1 oz
	the rind of 1 lemon, cut off thinly with a sharp knife	
25 g	light brown sugar	1 oz
1	whole egg	1
1	egg yolk	1
20 g	granulated sugar	1 oz
400 mL	milk	14 fl oz

Butter a baking dish then butter the bread. Cut the slices of bread in four. Put a layer of bread in the bottom of the dish, cover it with half the fruits, lemon peel and brown sugar. Cover this with another layer of bread, another layer of fruits, etc., and the final layer of bread.

Beat the egg with the egg yolk, most of the granulated sugar and the milk. Pour this mixture carefully down the side of the dish (not over the top of the bread) and leave to soak for a couple of hours.

To cook, sprinkle the last of the sugar over the top of the pudding and bake it in a moderately cool oven -160°C / 325°F - for 30 - 45 minutes or until the custard is set and the top is brown and crispy. Serve warm.

PER SERVING	
Energy Kcals	227.75
Protein g	7.33
Fat g	9.32
Saturated fatty acids g	4.73
Monounsaturated fatty acids g	2.81
Polyunsaturated fatty acids g	0.67
Carbohydrate g	30.87
Total Sugars g	17.10
Sodium mg	267.98
Fibre g	1.33

You can vary the texture of the pudding quite dramatically by varying the marmalade - from the darkish one with lots of peel, which I like, to a very pale one with very thin slivers of peel.

Steamed Marmalade Pudding

Serves 6

You can also steam the pudding in a microwave for 8 - 10 minutes on High although I never think microwaved puddings are quite as light.

100 g	low-fat spread or butter	4 oz
50 g	dark brown sugar	2 oz
2	eggs	2
100 g	sifted gram/chick pea flour	4 oz
5 mL, hpd	wheat- and gluten-free baking powder	1 hpd tsp
150 g	dark marmalade with largish chunks of peel	5½ oz
200 g	Greek yogurt, gluten free	7 oz
	juice of 1 lemon	
	juice of 1 orange	

Beat the butter or spread with the sugar. Beat in the eggs accompanying each with 15 mL /1 tablespoon of flour. Fold in the rest of the flour with the baking powder and the marmalade. Spoon the mixture into a well-greased bowl (it should come about ²/₃ of the way up) and cover it tightly with greaseproof paper held in place with string or a rubber band.

Put the bowl in a large saucepan so that the pudding has room to rise. Carefully pour water into the saucepan until it comes about half way up the bowl. Cover the pan, bring back to the boil and simmer up to 2 hours.

For the sauce, carefully mix the fruit juices into the yogurt.

To serve, turn the pudding onto a warmed serving plate and pour the sauce over before serving.

PER SERVING	
Energy Kcals	287.33
Protein g	9.07
Fat g	13.12
Saturated fatty acids g	4.57
Monounsaturated fatty acids g	5.22
Polyunsaturated fatty acids g	2.77
Carbohydrate g	36.73
Total Sugars g	28.72
Sodium mg	233.02
Fibre g	1.96

Fresh cranberries are very high in vitamin C.

Cranberry Rice Pudding

Serves 4

An interesting variation on a standard rice pud. If you do not like coconut milk you can use regular cow's milk but in that case you will need to sweeten it with 1 - 2 dessert spoons of sugar. The coconut and rice milks are both naturally very sweet so no extra sugar is needed.

50 g	short-grained pudding rice	2 oz
30 g	cranberries	1 oz
300 mL	coconut or rice milk	½ pint
	1 vanilla pod or 3 drops vanilla	

If you are using the vanilla pod, put it in the milk and bring it just to the boil, then allow to cool.

Put the rice, cranberries and milk (discarding the vanilla pod if used or with the vanilla extract if you are not using a pod) into an ovenproof dish. Mix and put in a low oven 150°C/ 300°F uncovered. Cook very slowly for 2½ - 3 hours, stirring whenever you happen to remember.

Serve warm or cold, alone or with cream, yogurt or ice cream.

PER SERVING	
Energy Kcals	62.50
Protein g	1.18
Fat g	0.30
Saturated fatty acids g	0.23
Monounsaturated fatty acids g	0.83
Polyunsaturated fatty acids g	0.83
Carbohydrate g	13.91
Total Sugars g	4.06
Sodium mg	82.65
Fibre g	0.98

If you prefer a biscuity base to the cheesecake, you could use the recipe for lemon shortbread or ginger biscuits, crumble them then mix them with 60 mL/ 4 tablespoons of melted butter. Press this mixture into the bottom of the tin to make the base.

Lemon Cheesecake

Serves 6

Since this cheesecake contains uncooked egg you should not feed it to children, pregnant women or elderly people.

¹/₂	a rice flour sponge cake (see page 180) cut in half horizontally	¹/₂
10 g	gelatin	¹/₃ oz
	grated rind and juice of 2 lemons	
225 g	ricotta cheese	8 oz
75 g	granulated sugar	3 oz
200 mL	whipping cream	7 fl oz
2	eggs, separated	2
50 g	golden raisins	2 oz

Lay half the sponge out on the bottom of a loose-bottomed cake tin.

Soak the gelatin in the lemon juice, heat it until the gelatin dissolves, then cool. Mix the lemon rind, ricotta cheese, sugar, cream, egg yolks and gelatin together thoroughly. Whisk the egg whites until they hold their shape in soft peaks; fold the whites into the cheese mixture along with the raisins. Spoon the mixture over the sponge cake and chill for at least four hours. Unmould, with the sponge on the bottom, from the cake tin onto a serving dish.

PER SERVING	
Energy Kcals	472.85
Protein g	11.57
Fat g	30.52
Saturated fatty acids g	17.99
Monounsaturated fatty acids g	8.94
Polyunsaturated fatty acids g	1.70
Carbohydrate g	42.19
Total Sugars g	36.11
Sodium mg	198.79
Fibre g	1.55

Fruit Crumbles

Serves 6

Fruit crumbles can be made with any combination or variety of fruits that you fancy. In each case they need to be gently stewed with a little water and a sweetener of your choice (sugar, dark brown sugar, honey, fruit concentrate, etc.). Drain off any extra juice before you put them into the baking dish and reserve it to be served with the crumble. If there is too much juice it will make the topping soggy.

Toppings can also be widely varied. You can use nuts or seeds as we have in the recipe below. Alternatively, you may want a more conventional crumble topping. In that case mix together:

75 g	sifted gram / chick pea flour	3 oz
50 g	rice flour	2 oz
75 g	granulated or light brown sugar	3 oz
50 g	butter or low-fat spread	2 oz

Rub the butter or low-fat spread into the flours. Mix in the sugar. Once the mixture is really sandy, spread it over the fruit in the baking dish and return to a moderate oven for 30 minutes to crisp the top.

Rhubarb Crumble

Serves 6

750 g	rhubarb, trimmed and chopped	1 lb 10 oz
30 mL	pear and apple concentrate or spread or dark brown sugar	2 tbsp
50 g	raisins	2 oz
100 mL	water	3½ fl oz
75 mL	chopped hazelnuts	5 tbsp
15 mL	sesame seeds	1 tbsp
15 mL	sunflower seeds	1 tbsp

PER SERVING	
Energy Kcals	160.95
Protein g	4.32
Fat g	6.26
Saturated fatty acids g	1.91
Monounsaturated fatty acids g	2.99
Polyunsaturated fatty acids g	4.13
Carbohydrate g	23.42
Total Sugars g	16.56
Sodium mg	14.48
Fibre g	3.35

For anyone who finds kiwi fruit too sweet raw, cooking them even very lightly for a minute in the microwave brings out their sharpness amazingly.

Clean and cut up the rhubarb. Put it in a saucepan with the pear and apple spread, raisins and water. Bring gently to the boil and simmer for 5 - 10 minutes or until the rhubarb is nearly soft. Transfer to a baking dish and drain off, reserving some of the juices, if it looks too runny. Mix together the hazelnuts, sesame and sunflower seeds and sprinkle them over the top of the rhubarb. Bake in a moderate oven (180°C/350°F) for 15 - 20 minutes or until the topping is lightly browned. Serve with the extra juice and cream, yogurt or ice cream.

Baked Fruit Flan

Serves 4

You could use any combination of fruit in this pie crust, but make sure that they have a good, sharp flavour. Mandarin sections, for example, might be rather bland.

50 g	rice flour	2 oz
75 g	sifted gram/chick pea flour	3 oz
50 g	low-fat spread	2 oz
45 mL	water	3 tbsp
15 mL	apple and pear concentrate or spread	1 tbsp
1	cooking apple	1
1	large orange	1
2	kiwi fruit	2
125 g	Greek yogurt, gluten free	4½ oz
25 g	browned, flaked almonds	1 oz

Heat the oven to 180°C / 350°F.

Rub the spread into the flours, then add enough water to make a soft dough. Roll out the pastry carefully and line a 15 cm (6 inch) round or oval pie dish. Line with foil or greaseproof paper and weight with beans. Bake for 10 minutes, then remove the foil and return to the oven for another 10 minutes to crisp the pastry.

Spread the pear and apple concentrate over the bottom of the pie crust.

Peel and slice the apple and lay it over the concentrate. Peel and thinly slice the orange and lay it over the apple, then do the same

PER SERVING	
Energy Kcals	287.94
Protein g	9.61
Fat g	12.82
Saturated fatty acids g	4.29
Monounsaturated fatty acids g	6.34
Polyunsaturated fatty acids g	3.34
Carbohydrate g	34.66
Total Sugars g	15.55
Sodium mg	117.31
Fibre g	4.76

Sweet omelettes are greatly underused. If you do not like rum, or you are feeding it to children, substitute water for the rum and fill the omelette with a jam of your choice.

with the kiwi fruit. Cover with foil and bake in the oven for a further 20 minutes. Remove from the oven, allow to cool slightly, then spread the yogurt over the fruit and sprinkle over the flaked almonds. Serve warm or at room temperature.

Sweet Rum Omelette

Serves 6

A great Victorian favourite, the omelette is quick to make and delicious.

6	medium eggs	6
90 mL	dark rum	6 tbsp
75 g	dark brown sugar	3 oz
30 mL	sunflower oil	2 tbsp

Whisk the eggs very thoroughly in a bowl with 50 g (2 oz) of the sugar and 45 mL / 3 tablespoons of the rum - you want a generally frothy mixture. Heat the omelette pan with a little butter or sunflower oil until it is very hot, pour in the omelette mixture and cook as for an ordinary omelette. If you are doing two small omelettes it would be better to cook them both at the same time, then turn them out onto the serving dish. Sprinkle them with the remaining sugar, warm the remaining rum, light it and pour it over the omelettes as they are carried to the table. If you are making one big one you will have to put the pan under a hot broiler to finish the top, then sprinkle the sugar and lighted rum over the omelette in the pan and serve it straight to the table.

PER SERVING	
Energy Kcals	211.70
Protein g	7.71
Fat g	11.48
Saturated fatty acids g	2.46
Monounsaturated fatty acids g	3.85
Polyunsaturated fatty acids g	3.89
Carbohydrate g	13.41
Total Sugars g	13.41
Sodium mg	88.08
Fibre g	0.00

When pears are out of season you could substitute a 400 g can of pineapple chunks, well drained.

Upside Down Ginger and Pear Pudding

Serves 8

This dessert tastes especially good as it is sweetened entirely by dried fruit with their rich and complex flavours.

50 g	crystallized ginger	2 oz
100 g	dates, dried	4 oz
1	large banana	1
150 g	butter or low-fat spread	5 oz
2.5 mL	nutmeg	½ tsp
2.5 mL	ground cinnamon	½ tsp
5 mL	ground ginger	1 tsp
3	eggs	3
175 g	chick pea (gram) flour	6 oz
500 g	pears	1 lb 2 oz

Heat the oven to 180°C/350°F.

Soak the ginger in boiling water for 15 minutes to remove most of the sugar, then rinse and chop it finely.

Purée the dates with the banana in a food processor, transfer to a mixer, add the butter and beat until relatively light and fluffy. Add the spices, then slowly beat in the eggs, adding a spoonful of flour with each one. Remove from the mixer and fold in the rest of the flour. If the mixture is dry, add a little milk or apple juice. Spoon a thin layer of the cake mix over the bottom of a well-greased 20 cm (8 inch) tin - round or square as you choose. Peel and core the pears and lay them, in a pattern, rounded side down, in the base of the tin. Carefully spoon in the rest of the cake mix and smooth off the top.

Bake for 30 - 35 minutes or until skewer comes out clean. Turn onto a warmed serving dish and serve with goat or sheep yogurt or ice cream.

PER SERVING	
Energy Kcals	244.19
Protein g	9.03
Fat g	11.41
Saturated fatty acids g	3.61
Monounsaturated fatty acids g	5.37
Polyunsaturated fatty acids g	3.49
Carbohydrate g	28.43
Total Sugars g	17.56
Sodium mg	165.92
Fibre g	4.30

Baking - Cookies, Cakes and Breads

Macaroons

Cheese Scones

Chocolate Brownies

Blueberry and Cranberry Muffins

Passion Cake

Chocolate Puffs

Lemon Shortbread

Chocolate Cake

Apple and Cinnamon Cake

Madeira Cake

Gooey Gingercake

Banana Bread

Ginger Cake

Walnut and Coffee Sponge

Aunt Vi's Ginger Cookies

Light Sponge or Angel Cake

Gram Flour Sponge Cake

Lemon Polenta Cake with Sunflower Seeds

Light Fruit Cake

Yorkshire Puddings

Rice and Corn "Soda" Bread

"Wholemeal" Brown Loaf

Wholemeal Bread with Pine Nuts and Walnuts

Stollen Bread

White Yeast Loaf

Doves Farm White Rice Loaf

Like meringues, you can also spread out the macaroon mix flat on rice paper on the base of a baking tray and use it as the base for a dessert.

Macaroons

Serves 20

If your macaroons go flat on you (which they often do...) they are excellent, broken up, as a topping for ice cream!

200 g	ground almonds	7 oz
200 g	granulated sugar	7 oz
3	egg whites	3
25 g	arrowroot	1 oz
2	drops vanilla	2
8	split almonds	8
	rice paper	

Heat the oven to 180°C/ 350°F.

Beat together the ground almonds, sugar, egg whites, arrowroot and vanilla until they are very well amalgamated. If they seem rather runny, add a little extra ground almond. Line a baking tray with rice paper cut to size.

Use a teaspoon to put 8 macaroons on the rice paper (if you have extra, make extra macaroons) and press a split almond into the top of each.

Bake the macaroons for approximately 10 minutes or until they are lightly browned and crisp on the outside.

Cool completely before storing in a tin.

PER SERVING	
Energy Kcals	263.63
Protein g	6.02
Fat g	11.66
Saturated fatty acids g	1.12
Monounsaturated fatty acids g	7.25
Polyunsaturated fatty acids g	3.08
Carbohydrate g	36.74
Total Sugars g	33.85
Sodium mg	33.08
Fibre g	1.53

If you want to make the scones really cheesey, grate some extra cheese on top before you put them in the oven.

Cheese Scones

Serves 6

These scones are good when fresh but do not keep very well - so eat them on the day they are made.

50 g	sifted chick pea (gram) flour	2 oz
75 g	rice flour	3 oz
	salt	
5 mL, hpd	wheat- and gluten-free baking powder	1 hpd tsp
75 g	Cheddar cheese, grated	3 oz
25 g	low-fat spread	1 oz
75-90mL	milk	5-6 tbsp
15 mL	squeeze fresh lemon juice	1 tbsp

Preheat the oven to 200°C/400°F.

Mix the dry ingredients together, then rub in the fat as though for pastry. Sour the milk with a squeeze of lemon juice, then mix it into the dry ingredients to make a moist dough.

Knead the dough lightly on a floured board, then press it out to approximately 4 cm/1 ½ inches thickness and cut out rounds (with a pastry cutter or a glass) or triangles.

Lay the scones on a floured baking tray and cook them in a hot oven for 7 - 15 minutes, depending on how large you have made them. They should be lightly browned but not burned. Cool on a rack.

PER SERVING	
Energy Kcals	151.57
Protein g	6.44
Fat g	7.22
Saturated fatty acids g	3.65
Monounsaturated fatty acids g	2.21
Polyunsaturated fatty acids g	0.85
Carbohydrate g	15.21
Total Sugars g	1.10
Sodium mg	247.65
Fibre g	1.14

Children may prefer the brownies without the walnuts.

Chocolate Brownies

Makes 12 brownies

A good rich brownie recipe.

150 g	low-fat spread	5 oz
150 g	dark brown sugar	5 oz
50 g	cocoa powder	2 oz
100 g	sifted chick pea (gram) flour	3½ oz
50 g	buckwheat flour	2 oz
15 mL	wheat- and gluten-free baking powder	3 tsp
150 mL	milk	5 fl oz
50 g	broken walnuts	2 oz

Preheat the oven to 160°C/325°F.

With an electric mixer beat the spread thoroughly with the sugar and the cocoa.

Fold in the flours and baking powder alternately with the milk, then fold in the walnuts.

Spoon the mixture into a well-oiled square (15cm x 15cm / 6 inch x 6 inch) or rectangular tin, smooth out with a spatula and bake for 30 minutes or until a skewer comes out clean.

Cool for a few minutes in the tin, then cut into whatever sized brownies you fancy.

Remove them carefully from the tin with a spatula and cool on a rack.

PER SERVING	
Energy Kcals	189.65
Protein g	4.22
Fat g	9.96
Saturated fatty acids g	2.49
Monounsaturated fatty acids g	3.20
Polyunsaturated fatty acids g	3.37
Carbohydrate g	22.77
Total Sugars g	13.65
Sodium mg	193.92
Fibre g	1.47

If you cannot find fresh blueberries or cranberries, you could use plump raisins or sultanas, or even chocolate buttons.

Blueberry and Cranberry Muffins

Serves 6

Delicious for a lazy Sunday morning breakfast with the papers…

75 g	low-fat spread	3 oz
40 g	light brown sugar	1½ oz
1	small egg	1
120 mL	milk	4 fl oz
75 g	sifted chick pea (gram) flour	3 oz
75 g	rice flour	3 oz
5 mL, hpd	wheat- and gluten-free baking powder	1 hpd tsp
	small pinch salt	
2.5 mL	vanilla	½ tsp
40 g	cranberries	1½ oz
40 g	blueberries	1½ oz

Heat the oven to 180°C / 350°F.

Beat the low-fat spread, sugar, egg and milk together with an electric beater.

Mix the flours with the baking powder and salt and gradually beat them into the liquid mixture. Fold in the vanilla, cranberries and blueberries and spoon the dough into a greased muffin pan. Bake the muffins for 20 minutes or until they are risen and firm to the touch. Remove them and cool them slightly on a rack. The muffins are also good cold and freeze well.

PER SERVING	
Energy Kcals	187.02
Protein g	5.77
Fat g	7.54
Saturated fatty acids g	2.33
Monounsaturated fatty acids g	3.02
Polyunsaturated fatty acids g	1.77
Carbohydrate g	24.95
Total Sugars g	8.88
Sodium mg	235.57
Fibre g	1.91

Passion Cake

This passion cake is sweetened only by dates which adds to its flavour without making it too sweet.

3	medium eggs	3
100 g	dried, stoned dates, (soaked in boiling water if they are very hard,) and chopped	4 oz
100 g	low-fat spread	4 oz
150 g	carrots, grated	5 oz
150 g	ripe pears, peeled, cored and puréed in a food processor	5 oz
150 g	chick pea (gram) flour	5 oz
10 mL, hpd	gluten-free baking powder	2 hpd tsp
10 mL	ground cinnamon	2 level tsp
5 mL	ground nutmeg	1 level tsp
2.5 mL	ground allspice	½ level tsp
	pinch salt	
200 g	ricotta cheese	7 oz
30 mL	pear and apple spread	2 tbsp
1	grated rind of 1 orange	1

Preheat the oven to 190°C/375°F.

Whisk the eggs, dates and low-fat spread together in a processor until they are creamy. Mix in the carrots and pears. Sift together the flour, baking powder and spices, then fold them into the liquid mixture, making sure they are thoroughly amalgamated. Pour into a buttered and floured 20 cm/8 inch cake tin, with a removable bottom and bake in a moderately hot oven for 25 minutes or until the cake is firm to the touch. Remove from the oven and allow to cool on a wire rack.

The cake can be eaten perfectly well as it is, but if you want to ice it, heat the pear and apple spread until it is just runny and mix it into the ricotta cheese along with the orange rind. Spread over the cake and allow to cool.

FOR THE WHOLE CAKE	
Energy Kcals	1801.78
Protein g	77.05
Fat g	84.52
Saturated fatty acids g	28.68
Monounsaturated fatty acids g	35.40
Polyunsaturated fatty acids g	19.60
Carbohydrate g	199.65
Total Sugars g	126.34
Sodium mg	2198.93
Fibre g	27.25

If you have a piping bag you can have great fun piping meringue into all kinds of fun shapes - animals, hearts, golf clubs - anything you want. Just be very careful, especially if you have thin pieces like legs, when you take them off the foil, that you do not break them.

Chocolate Puffs

Makes 20 puffs

These are delightful little chocolate meringues - excellent on their own or as an accompaniment to a dessert.

1	large egg white	1
100 g	fine granulated sugar	4 oz
25 g	plain chocolate, grated	1 oz

Beat the egg white until very stiff. Then beat in the sugar and grated chocolate; the mixture will go rather runny in the process but it does not matter. Line a baking sheet with foil. Grease the foil and drop very small teaspoonfuls of the mixture onto it, allowing a certain amount of room for each puff to spread. You should get around 20 puffs from the mixture.

Bake the puffs in a cool oven (110°C / 225°F) for an hour or until they are completely dried out. Gently pry them off the foil and store in an airtight box ready for use.

PER SERVING	
Energy Kcals	53.97
Protein g	0.58
Fat g	0.77
Saturated fatty acids g	0.46
Monounsaturated fatty acids g	0.27
Polyunsaturated fatty acids g	0.07
Carbohydrate g	12.16
Total Sugars g	12.03
Sodium mg	8.38
Fibre g	0.00

You could use these as a base for strawberry shortbreads. Just mix fresh strawberries into some lightly whipped and sweetened cream and pile them on top.

Lemon Shortbread

Makes about 12 biscuits

These shortbread are crumblier than those made with wheat flour so need careful handling - but they do taste excellent.

50 g	butter	2 oz
75 g	pale brown sugar	3 oz
	grated rind of 1 lemon	
50 g	ground almonds	2 oz
100 g	sifted chick pea /gram flour	4 oz

Beat the butter with the sugar with an electric whisk until soft and light. Add the lemon rind, then rub in the ground almonds and gram flour with your fingers, working as lightly as you can. Pat the mixture out into the bottom of a greased tin or shape it into a round approximately 2 cm (^{1}/$_2$ inch) thick. Score the mixture with a knife into sections. Bake it in a moderate oven (160°C/325°F) for 15 minutes.

Remove and cut the break points (it should make around 12 biscuits) with a knife then return to the oven for another 5 minutes. Cool slightly then cut along the score marks, remove carefully, with a spatula, to a rack and leave to get quite cold.

PER SERVING	
Energy Kcals	106.85
Protein g	2.62
Fat g	6.18
Saturated fatty acids g	2.49
Monounsaturated fatty acids g	2.36
Polyunsaturated fatty acids g	0.93
Carbohydrate g	11.02
Total Sugars g	6.92
Sodium mg	35.88
Fibre g	1.20

You could also use this mixture to make individual chocolate cup cakes but you would need to reduce the cooking time to around 15 minutes.

Chocolate Cake

A classic chocolate cake - a great favourite with children. It usually is eaten before it gets a chance to be iced, but if you wish to ice it you could do so with a standard chocolate butter icing or just with melted chocolate, milk or plain.

150 g	low-fat spread or butter	5 oz
170 g	dark brown sugar	6 oz
50 g	cocoa powder	2 oz
100 mL	boiling water	3½ fl oz
3	medium eggs	3
150 g	rice flour, brown if possible	5 oz
10 mL, hpd	wheat- and gluten-free baking powder	2 hpd tsp

Heat the oven to 180°C / 350°F.

With an electric mixer beat the spread or butter with the sugar until they are light and fluffy. Meanwhile, mix the cocoa powder with the boiling water until you have a smooth paste. Beat the cocoa into the mixture, then slowly beat in the three eggs, each accompanied by a spoonful of flour. Fold in the rest of the flour with the baking powder.

Pour the mixture into a well-greased 15 cm or 20 cm (6 or 8 inch) round cake tin with a removable bottom and bake for 30 minutes or until it is firm to the touch and a skewer comes out clean from the middle. Cool slightly, then turn onto a rack to get cold before cutting.

FOR THE WHOLE CAKE	
Energy Kcals	2709.80
Protein g	42.34
Fat g	153.99
Saturated fatty acids g	65.83
Monounsaturated fatty acids g	61.56
Polyunsaturated fatty acids g	16.41
Carbohydrate g	305.19
Total Sugars g	176.11
Sodium mg	3167.20
Fibre g	9.05

This cake keeps excellently either in a tin or in the fridge.

Apple and Cinnamon Cake

A delicious moist and spicy light fruit cake.

100 g	low-fat spread	4 oz
200 g	dried dates, finely chopped	7 oz
225 g	tart eating apples, cored, peeled and grated	8 oz
10 mL, hpd	ground cinnamon	2 hpd tsp
5 mL	ground mixed spice	1 level tsp
	pinch salt	
75 g	raisins	3 oz
2	medium eggs, beaten	2
175 mL	milk	6 fl oz
125 g	rice flour	4 oz
125 g	sifted chick pea (gram) flour	4 oz
10 mL, hpd	baking powder	2 hpd tsp

Preheat the oven to 180°C/350°F and grease and line a 20 cm / 8 inch square tin. Put low-fat spread, dates, apple, cinnamon, mixed spice and salt into a processor and blend thoroughly. Fold in the raisins and eggs alternately with the flour, baking powder and milk. When all are amalgamated, transfer them into the prepared tin.

Bake for 30 - 40 minutes until dark golden and firm to the touch. Test with a skewer. Remove from the oven and leave to cool in the tin for 10 - 15 minutes before turning onto a wire rack to cool completely.

FOR THE WHOLE CAKE	
Energy Kcals	2410.63
Protein g	69.73
Fat g	69.52
Saturated fatty acids g	22.26
Monounsaturated fatty acids g	29.08
Polyunsaturated fatty acids g	19.31
Carbohydrate g	392.58
Total Sugars g	225.14
Sodium mg	2139.01
Fibre g	29.39

It is important to toss the cherries in the flour if you do not want them all to sink to the bottom of the cake. Or maybe you prefer a cake with a layer of cherries at the bottom!

Madeira Cake

Plain madeira cake is always a great favourite, whether served with a glass of madeira or a cup of tea! Adding the cherries might be appropriate for a more festive occasion.

175 g	butter	7 oz
150 g	granulated sugar	6 oz
	grated rind and juice of 1 lemon	
	pinch ground cinnamon	
3	medium eggs	3
4	drops vanilla	4
90 g	sifted chick pea (gram) flour	3 oz
90 g	rice flour	3½ oz
5 mL, hpd	wheat- and gluten-free baking powder	1 hpd tsp
100 g	glacé cherries (optional)	4 oz

Preheat the oven to 160°C / 325°F.

Cream the butter with the sugar until they are light and fluffy. Add the lemon rind and the cinnamon. Beat in the eggs, one at a time, adding a little flour with each.

Toss the cherries (if you are using them) in the remains of the flours then fold them into the mixture along with the flours, vanilla and the lemon juice. If the mixture is too thick, add a little milk.

Spoon the mixture into a greased, loose-bottomed or lined 18 cm/7 inch tin and bake for 40 - 50 minutes or until a skewer comes out clean.

Remove from the oven and turn out onto a rack to cool.

FOR THE WHOLE CAKE INCLUDING CHERRIES	
Energy Kcals	3016.54
Protein g	49.12
Fat g	169.64
Saturated fatty acids g	102.13
Monounsaturated fatty acids g	45.70
Polyunsaturated fatty acids g	10.74
Carbohydrate g	346.27
Total Sugars g	230.78
Sodium mg	1993.33
Fibre g	12.39

The gingerbread is even better served warm as a dessert with vanilla ice cream.

Gooey Gingercake

This is a seriously, wonderfully gooey cake, based on a recipe given to me many years ago by a colleague's Scottish mother - and in the original it was even sweeter and even gooier!

100 g	butter	4 oz
100 g	dark brown sugar	4 oz
300 g	molasses	10½ oz
3	medium eggs	3
225 g	brown rice flour	8 oz
5 mL	gluten- and wheat-free baking powder	1 tsp
5 mL	ground ginger	1 tsp
5 mL, hpd	gluten-free pumpkin pie spice	1 hpd tsp
5 mL, hpd	cinnamon	1 hpd tsp

Melt the butter, sugar and molasses together in a pan or microwave. Remove from heat. Beat the eggs into the melted mixture followed by the flour and spices. Pour it (the mixture will be very runny) into a greased loaf tin or cake tin (the size will depend on whether you want a small, deep cake or a larger, flatter one) and bake in a moderately cool oven (160°C / 325°F) for an hour. Take out of the oven, remove from the tin and cool on a rack. Serve it sliced, by itself or buttered.

FOR THE WHOLE CAKE	
Energy Kcals	2966.52
Protein g	41.43
Fat g	103.09
Saturated fatty acids g	59.62
Monounsaturated fatty acids g	28.28
Polyunsaturated fatty acids g	4.78
Carbohydrate g	487.88
Total Sugars g	306.12
Sodium mg	1569.45
Fibre g	4.50

You can eat the bread on its own or with butter - or real banana fans use it for banana sandwiches.

Banana Bread

A wonderful way to use up those over-ripe bananas that no one will eat.

100 g	low-fat spread	4 oz
2	medium eggs	2
15 mL	milk	3 tbsp
225 g	chick pea (gram) flour, sifted	8 oz
5 mL	baking soda	1 tsp
3	large, very ripe bananas	3

Preheat the oven to 180°C/350°F.
   Beat the spread with the eggs and milk until they are pale and fluffy. Sift the flour with the baking soda and add it alternately with the eggs. Mash the bananas and add them to the mixture with extra milk if it is too stiff. Spoon the mixture into a greased 450 g/ 1 lb loaf tin and bake in a moderate oven for 1 - 1 ½ hours or until a skewer comes out clean. Cool on a rack.

FOR THE WHOLE CAKE	
Energy Kcals	1560.65
Protein g	68.88
Fat g	66.66
Saturated fatty acids g	16.60
Monounsaturated fatty acids g	30.72
Polyunsaturated fatty acids g	18.37
Carbohydrate g	184.60
Total Sugars g	72.10
Sodium mg	1512.85
Fibre g	27.73

If you are only a moderate ginger enthusiast you could leave out the stem ginger pieces and substitute 5 mL / 1 heaped teaspoon of ground ginger.

Ginger Cake

A rich ginger cake with delicious lumps of stem ginger - for real ginger enthusiasts.

100 g	butter or low-fat spread	4 oz
50 g	dark brown sugar	2 oz
100 g	maple syrup	4 oz
3	medium eggs	3
125g	buckwheat flour	4 1/2 oz
100 g	rice flour	4 oz
10 mL, hpd	ground ginger	2 hpd tsp
5 mL, hpd	ground cinnamon	1 hpd tsp
5 mL	ground nutmeg	1 tsp
50 g	stem ginger pieces, chopped	2 oz
100 mL	apple juice, unsweetened	4 fl oz

Beat the butter or spread with the sugar until it is soft and light. Beat in the maple syrup, then slowly beat in the 3 eggs alternately with the buckwheat flour. Fold in the rice flour, spices and ginger pieces along with enough apple juice to keep the mixture moist. Spoon it into a 15 / 20 cm (6 or 8 inch) greased round cake tin and bake for 35 - 40 minutes in a moderate oven (180°C/350°F) or until a skewer comes out clean. Turn out of the tin and cool on a rack.

FOR THE WHOLE CAKE	
Energy Kcals	1991.08
Protein g	46.35
Fat g	64.24
Saturated fatty acids g	19.49
Monounsaturated fatty acids g	28.23
Polyunsaturated fatty acids g	13.27
Carbohydrate g	323.48
Total Sugars g	126.44
Sodium mg	942.89
Fibre g	5.63

If you wanted you could cover the cake with a caramel butter icing but I feel that it is quite rich enough the way it is.

Walnut and Coffee Sponge

This cake tastes excellent with its large pieces of walnut - and keeps very well in a tightly fitting tin or covered with plastic wrap.

150 g	butter or low fat spread	5 oz
150 g	dark brown sugar	5 oz
3	medium eggs	3
150 g	chick pea (gram) flour	5 oz
150 g	rice flour	5 oz
5 mL	ground nutmeg	1 tsp
5 mL	ground cinnamon	1 tsp
2.5 mL	ground cloves	½ tsp
	small pinch of salt	
10 mL, hpd	gluten- and wheat-free baking powder	2 hpd tsp
300 mL	strong black coffee	½ pint
150 g	chopped walnuts	5 oz

Heat the oven to 180°C / 350°F.

Beat the butter or spread with the sugar until it is fairly light and fluffy.

Separate the eggs and beat the 3 egg yolks into the mixture. Sift the flour with the spices, salt and baking powder, then add it to the butter and sugar mixture alternately with the coffee. Stir in the chopped walnuts. Whisk the egg whites until they hold their shape but are not stiff or dry and mix and fold them carefully into the cake mixture. Spoon it into a 20 cm / 8 inch round cake tin - or a similar capacity loaf tin - with a loose bottom or lined with greaseproof paper.

Bake for 50 - 60 minutes or until a skewer comes out clean. Remove from the oven and the tin and cool on a rack.

FOR THE WHOLE CAKE	
Energy Kcals	3979.38
Protein g	85.77
Fat g	258.09
Saturated fatty acids g	99.31
Monounsaturated fatty acids g	61.48
Polyunsaturated fatty acids g	84.38
Carbohydrate g	357.92
Total Sugars g	163.11
Sodium mg	2602.74
Fibre g	24.30

Right:
Yorkshire Puddings
(page 184)

These are particularly delicious served with a stewed fruit such as rhubarb.

Aunt Vi's Ginger Cookies

Makes around 12 cookies

As with all cookies free of wheat flour, these are pretty crumbly so need to be treated with care. But they are delicious so it is worth the effort!

40 g	light brown sugar	1½ oz
50 g	rice flour	2 oz
40 g	gram / chick pea flour	1½ oz
10 mL	ground ginger	2 tsp
	pinch of salt	
75 g	butter	3 oz

Mix the sugar, flours, ginger and salt in a bowl then rub in the butter - you can use a pastry mixer for this. Press the mixture out into a greased baking tin about 2 cm / ½ inch thick and bake it for 10 minutes in a moderately hot oven (160°C/325°F). Take the tray out and cut the mixture into cookie shapes - return to the oven for a further 5 minutes or until the cookies are golden. Remove from the oven and leave to cool. They can be dusted with sifted icing sugar or a little sprinkling of ground ginger.

PER BISCUIT	
Energy Kcals	87.94
Protein g	1.04
Fat g	5.34
Saturated fatty acids g	3.40
Monounsaturated fatty g	1.28
Polyunsaturated fatty acids g	0.26
Carbohydrate g	9.35
Total Sugars g	3.61
Sodium mg	81.98
Fibre g	0.46

Left:
"Wholemeal" Brown Loaf (page 186);
Middle: White Yeast Loaf (page 189);
Bottom: Rice and Corn "Soda" Bread (page 185)

Light Sponge or Angel Cake

This is excellent on its own just sprinkled with a little icing sugar and layered with jam but it also makes a first-class base for a wide range of desserts.

6	medium eggs	6
150 g	fine granulated sugar	5 oz
150 g	rice flour	5 oz

Heat the oven to 160°C / 325°F.

Line a loose-bottomed 20 cm (8 inch) cake tin with lightly floured greaseproof paper.

Whisk the eggs and sugar together with an electric whisk until they are light and fluffy. Sift the flour into the bowl and fold it very carefully into the egg mixture making sure that you do not get any lumps of flour.

Pour the mixture into the tin and bake for 20 - 30 minutes or until the cake is firm to the touch.

Remove from the oven and, carefully, from the tin. Peel off the greaseproof paper and allow to cool on a rack.

If you are to use the cake in another recipe (trifle or tiramisu) and do not want to use it all, the remains will freeze well.

FOR THE WHOLE CAKE	
Energy Kcals	1669.20
Protein g	56.10
Fat g	40.08
Saturated fatty acids g	11.16
Monounsaturated fatty acids g	16.92
Polyunsaturated fatty acids g	4.32
Carbohydrate g	281.25
Total Sugars g	161.10
Sodium mg	519.00
Fibre g	3.00

Gram Flour Sponge Cake

Gram or chick pea flour makes a rather more substantial but still excellent cake to be eaten on its own or used as a base for other dishes.

200 g	butter	7 oz
200 g	light brown sugar	7 oz
3	medium eggs	3
200 g	sifted gram/chick pea flour	7 oz
10 mL	gluten- and wheat-free baking powder	2 tsp
5 mL	vanilla	1 tsp

Heat the oven to 180°C / 350°F.

Beat the butter with the sugar until light and fluffy. Beating slowly, add the eggs alternately with the flour. Fold in the remaining flour, baking powder and vanilla. Spoon into a well-oiled or lined 20 cm (8 inch) tin and bake it for 30 minutes or until the cake is firm to the touch and a skewer comes out clean. Cool on a rack and when cold, split and fill with jam of your choice. If you wish, you can also dust the top with icing sugar or soft brown sugar.

FOR THE WHOLE CAKE	
Energy Kcals	3093.49
Protein g	63.26
Fat g	193.67
Saturated fatty acids g	114.58
Monounsaturated fatty acids g	50.26
Polyunsaturated fatty acids g	12.76
Carbohydrate g	306.73
Total Sugars g	211.63
Sodium mg	2246.00
Fibre g	21.40

If you would rather a smooth cake, leave out the sunflower seeds.

Lemon Polenta Cake with Sunflower Seeds

The lemon juice makes this a deliciously refreshing cake with morning coffee.

50 g	sunflower seeds	2 oz
125 g	butter	5 oz
125 g	light brown sugar	5 oz
2	whole eggs	2
2	egg yolks	2
100 g	corn flour or polenta	4 oz
75 g	potato flour	3 oz
10 mL, hpd	gluten- and wheat-free baking powder	2 hpd tsp
	grated rind and juice of 2 lemons	
60 mL	sweet white wine	3 tbsp

Heat the oven to 180°C / 350°F.

Whizz the sunflower seeds in a food processor until they are well broken but not powdered. Toast them lightly in a dry pan until they brown lightly but do not let them burn. Cool.

Cream the butter with the sugar until light and fluffy. Add the eggs and egg yolks alternately with spoonfuls of the flours, beating slowly. By hand, fold in the rest of the flour and baking powder alternately with the lemon rind and juice, the sunflower seeds and the wine.

Spoon into a prepared 20 cm (8 inch) greased sandwich tin and bake for 30 minutes or until the cake is firm to the touch and a skewer comes out clean.

Cool on a rack before cutting.

FOR THE WHOLE CAKE	
Energy Kcals	2668.40
Protein g	50.58
Fat g	156.16
Saturated fatty acids g	77.30
Monounsaturated fatty acids g	43.32
Polyunsaturated fatty acids g	22.13
Carbohydrate g	278.22
Total Sugars g	141.68
Sodium mg	1796.50
Fibre g	7.28

Light Fruit Cake

This is a real fruit cake since the only sweeteners it contains are dried fruits. It makes quite a crumbly mixture so allow it to cool completely in the tin before turning it out.

100 g	low-fat spread or butter	4 oz
50 g	dried dates, softened in hot water	2 oz
1	medium banana	1
	rind and juice of 2 oranges	
	rind and juice of 1 lemon	
75 g	raisins	3 oz
50 g	currants	2 oz
25 g	mixed peel	1 oz
50 g	glacé cherries, halved	2 oz
100 g	ground almonds	4 oz
75 g	chick pea (gram) flour	3 oz
50 g	brown rice flour	2 oz
15 mL	gluten- and wheat-free baking powder	3 tsp
10 mL	ground nutmeg	2 tsp

Heat the oven to 160°C/325°F. Line a 20 cm/8 inch tin with oiled greaseproof paper.

Soften the low-fat spread or butter, then beat until creamy. Chop the dates in a food processor, then add the banana and purée. Beat this mixture into the creamed spread or butter, then beat in the orange and lemon juice and rind.

Fold in the raisins and currants, mixed peel, glacé cherries and ground almonds. Fold in the flours, baking powder and nutmeg and mix well. If the mixture is too dry, add a little milk or extra orange juice.

Spoon the mixture into the lined tin and bake for 50 minutes - 1 hour or until the skewer comes out clean.

FOR THE WHOLE CAKE	
Energy Kcals	2244.73
Protein g	51.73
Fat g	112.92
Saturated fatty acids g	21.48
Monounsaturated fatty acids g	59.27
Polyunsaturated fatty acids g	30.38
Carbohydrate g	276.27
Total Sugars g	196.91
Sodium mg	1676.24
Fibre g	22.82

Yorkshire Puddings

Serves 6

The pudding can be served with roast beef as normal or you can serve it by itself with gravy - or even as a dessert with jam!

50 g	chick pea (gram) flour	2 oz
50 g	rice flour	2 oz
1	egg	1
	salt and black pepper	
200 mL	milk	7 fl oz
30 mL	sunflower oil	2 tbsp

Heat the oven to 230°C / 450°F.

Put the flours, egg and milk, with a pinch of salt and a grind of black pepper, in the food processor and whizz thoroughly.

Pour a couple of drops of sunflower oil into the bottom of 12 individual muffin tins or one flat baking dish. Put in the oven for a couple of minutes to heat until the oil is smoking. Pour the batter into the individual holders or into the tin and return it to the oven at once. Bake for 20 minutes or until the puddings are risen and golden.

Serve at once with beef, with gravy - or with jam!

PER SERVING	
Energy Kcals	140.43
Protein g	4.67
Fat g	8.03
Saturated fatty acids g	1.83
Monounsaturated fatty acids g	1.99
Polyunsaturated fatty acids g	3.55
Carbohydrate g	12.67
Total Sugars g	2.08
Sodium mg	102.71
Fibre g	1.06

Rice and Corn "Soda" Bread

Another no-yeast bread which is quite dense in texture but very well flavoured.

150 g	potato flour	5 oz
150 g	rice flour	5 oz
50 g	buckwheat flour	2 oz
100 g	fine corn flour	4 oz
15 mL	soya flour	3 tsp
5 mL	baking soda	1 tsp
10 mL	cream of tartar	2 tsp
5 mL	sugar	1 tsp
3 mL	salt	3/4 tsp
7.5 mL	butter	1/2 tbsp
1	large egg, beaten	1
250 mL	milk	9 fl oz

Heat the oven to 180°C / 350°F.

Mix the flours together in a mixing bowl, then mix in the other dry ingredients. Rub in the butter, then stir in the egg and the milk, making sure that they are all thoroughly amalgamated.

Grease or oil a 15 cm / 6 inch round cake tin or loaf tin and pour in the soda bread mixture. Or form into a circle on a greased baking tray and cut a cross in the top. Bake in the centre of the oven for 45 - 50 minutes or until a skewer comes out clean.

Allow to cool slightly in the tin, covered with a tea towel, then knock out carefully onto the rack. Cover with a tea towel and allow to get completely cold before slicing.

PER LOAF	
Energy Kcals	2181.1
Protein g	65.45
Fat g	48.55
Saturated fatty acids g	23.9
Monounsaturated fatty acids g	13.44
Polyunsaturated fatty acids g	2.97
Carbohydrate g	379.38
Total Sugars g	33.76
Sodium mg	3462.35
Englyst fibre g	14.63

"Wholemeal" Brown Loaf

This is similar in taste and texture to a fairly dense wholemeal wheat loaf. The sesame seeds give a little extra interest - assuming that you are able to eat them - but are quite dispensable.

350 g	brown rice flour	12 oz
50 g	buckwheat flour	2 oz
50 g	potato flour	2 oz
5 mL	soya flour	1 tsp
2.5 mL	salt	1/2 tsp
10 mL	sugar	2 tsp
7.5 mL	cream of tartar	1 1/2 tsp
1 mL	baking soda	1/4 tsp
10 mL	quick rising yeast	2 tsp
7.5 mL	butter	1/2 tbsp
1	medium egg, beaten	1
7.5 mL	sesame seeds (optional)	1/2 tbsp
425 mL	warm water	15 fl oz

Heat oven to 180°C / 350°F. Grease a 1 kg /2 lb loaf tin or a round cake tin.

Mix all the dry ingredients (except the sesame seeds) thoroughly in a large mixing bowl. Rub in the butter, then stir in the egg and half the sesame seeds, if you are using them. Make up the 425 mL (15 fl oz) of warm water with 150 mL (5 fl oz) of boiling water, cooled with 275 mL (10 fl oz) of tap water. Stir this gradually into the dry mixture. This will make an extremely runny mixture, but do not worry, it will firm up in the baking.

Warm the tin and then pour in the mixture. Sprinkle over the remaining sesame seeds and bake it in the centre of the oven for 40 minutes or until it is risen and a skewer comes out clean.

Cool in the tin for 5 - 10 minutes under a tea towel then carefully knock out onto the rack. Cover with a tea towel and leave until it is quite cold before cutting.

FOR THE WHOLE LOAF

Energy Kcals	2028.73
Protein g	44.25
Fat g	37.74
Saturated fatty acids g	14.16
Monounsaturated fatty acids g	11.22
Polyunsaturated fatty acids g	6.65
Carbohydrate g	373.48
Total Sugars g	13.48
Sodium mg	2326.4
Fibre g	13.16

Wholemeal Bread with Pine Nuts and Walnuts

A "party" version of the plain "wholemeal" loaf.

300 g	brown rice flour	10 oz
100 g	corn meal	4 oz
50 g	buckwheat flour	2 oz
5 mL	soya flour	1 tsp
5 mL	salt	1 scant tsp
15 mL	gluten- and wheat-free baking powder	3 tsp
10 mL	sugar	2 tsp
2.5 mL	quick rising yeast	1/2 tsp
10 mL	sesame seeds	2 tsp
15 mL	chopped walnuts	1 tbsp
15 mL	pine nuts	1 tbsp
15 mL	butter	1 tbsp
1	egg, beaten	1
500 mL	warm water	18 fl oz

Heat the oven to 180°C / 350°F.
   Mix all the dry ingredients well together then rub in the butter. Stir in the egg. Add 350 mL (12 fl oz) of cold water to 150 mL (6 fl oz) of boiling and mix it into the dry mix. You will end up with a very sloppy mix. Grease or oil a 1 kg / 2 lb oblong or round loaf tin and pour in the mixture. Bake it in the centre of the oven for 50 - 60 minutes or until a skewer comes out clean. Cool for 5 minutes in the tin, covered with a tea towel then carefully knock it out onto a rack. Cover with a tea towel and leave to get completely cold before cutting.

FOR THE WHOLE LOAF	
Energy Kcals	2444.28
Protein g	56.15
Fat g	70.58
Saturated fatty acids g	16.41
Monounsaturated fatty acids g	17.65
Polyunsaturated fatty acids g	24.24
Carbohydrate g	390.52
Total Sugars g	13.93
Sodium mg	3589.15
Fibre g	13.95

Stollen Bread

Although this calls itself a bread and is based on a bread recipe it is really more of a cake texture than a bread. None the less, it tastes delicious!

300 g	rice flour	10 oz
50 g	sugar	2 oz
2.5 mL	salt	½ tsp
2.5 mL	quick rising yeast	½ tsp
5 mL	cream of tartar	1 tsp
2.5 mL	baking soda	½ tsp
15 mL	ground almonds	1 tbsp
30 mL	butter	2 tbsp
15 mL	mixed peel	1 tbsp
15 mL	glacé cherries, chopped	1 tbsp
15 mL	golden raisins	1 tbsp
	grated peel of 1 lemon	
15 mL	sunflower seeds, chopped roughly	1 tbsp
15 mL	pumpkin seeds, chopped roughly	1 tbsp
1	medium egg, beaten	1
120 mL	warm, 2% milk	4 fl oz

Heat the oven to 150°C / 300°F.

In a large bowl mix together the flour, salt, sugar, yeast, soda, cream of tartar and ground almonds. Rub in the fat then add the other dry ingredients. Mix in the egg and then the warm milk.

Spoon the mixture into a well greased 450 g / 1 lb loaf tin or round cake tin and bake in the centre of the oven for 30 - 35 minutes or until a skewer comes out clean. Remove from the oven and allow to cool for a few minutes in the tin, before turning out carefully, onto a rack. Cover with a tea towel and allow to cool completely before cutting.

Serve alone or with butter or jam.

FOR THE WHOLE LOAF	
Energy Kcals	2378.13
Protein g	50.72
Fat g	81.96
Saturated fatty acids g	25.34
Monounsaturated fatty acids g	27.62
Polyunsaturated fatty acids g	20.09
Carbohydrate g	358.52
Total Sugars g	109.74
Sodium mg	1580.40
Fibre g	12.60

Breads made with wheat flour have gluten to help hold them up once they have risen. Some breads made with rice flour or chick pea flour may sink a little when cooked. They may not look as good but they are just as, if not more, delicious to eat.

White Yeast Loaf

This makes an excellent light golden coloured loaf with a good texture.

300 g	rice flour	10 oz
75 g	corn flour	3 oz
5 mL	soya flour	1 tsp
2.5 mL	salt	½ tsp
1	package quick rising yeast	1
10 mL	sugar	2 tsp
5 mL	cream of tartar	1 tsp
2.5 mL	baking soda	½ tsp
15 mL	butter	1 tbsp
1	large egg, beaten	1
400 mL	warm water made up with ⅓ boiling water and ⅔ cold tap water	14 fl oz

In a large bowl mix all the dry ingredients together, then rub in the butter. Add the egg and water and stir well together to make a really sloppy mixture. Stir this very well (by hand, not in a mixer) until it is thoroughly amalgamated.

Grease and warm a 1 kg/ 2 lb tin and pour in the mixture. Cover it with greased aluminum foil and allow it to rise in a warm place for 20 minutes.

Heat the oven to 200°C / 400°F.

Remove the foil and bake for 10 minutes in the hot oven. Reduce the heat to 180°C / 350°F and continue to bake for a further 15 minutes by which time the loaf should be risen and a skewer comes out clean.

Cool the loaf for some minutes in the tin, then carefully knock it out onto a rack, cover with a cloth and allow to cool completely.

FOR THE WHOLE LOAF	
Energy Kcals	1678.43
Protein g	38.71
Fat g	28.16
Saturated fatty acids g	12.71
Monounsaturated fatty acids g	6.85
Polyunsaturated fatty acids g	1.42
Carbohydrate g	308.08
Total Sugars g	12.04
Sodium mg	1910.20
Fibre g	8.33

Doves Farm White Rice Loaf

This is an adaptation of a recipe developed by Doves Farm (who provide breads, biscuits and cakes for those on special diets) for their own rice flour. The best texture is achieved by part microwaving the bread and then baking it although it also works well (if you do not have a microwave) baking it in a pot of hot water (bain marie).

300 g	rice flour	10 oz
2 x 7g	package quick rising yeast	2 x 7g
15 mL	sugar	1 tbsp
5 mL	salt	1 tsp
300 mL	warm water made up of ⅓ boiling water and ⅔ cold tap water	½ pint
2	medium eggs, beaten	2
30 mL	sunflower oil	2 tbsp

Put the flour, yeast, sugar and salt in a mixing bowl, add the water and mix well. Add the eggs and oil and mix again. Pour the mixture into very well oiled containers:

1. 1.5 L (2 ½ pint) microwave container for the microwave version.

2. A 450 g (1 lb) loaf tin for the bain marie version. Cover with well-oiled foil and leave to rise for 20 minutes in a very warm place.

To bake:
1. Microwave. Uncover the bread, place it on a microwave baking tray and bake on High / 600 W for 6 minutes. Meanwhile heat the oven to 220°C/450°F.
   Remove the bread from the microwave, allow to cool for a few minutes then unmould onto a baking tray. Bake, uncovered for 10-15 minutes to give it a crust.
   Remove onto a baking rack, cover with a tea towel and allow to cool.

2. Oven: Preheat the oven to 220°C / 450°F. Sit the risen dough in the baking tin and pour boiling water round to half the tin height. Bake, covered for 10 minutes. Reduce the heat to 180°C / 350°F and bake for a further 20 minutes uncovered. Remove from the oven, allow to cool for a few minutes, then turn out of the tin onto a baking tray. Increase the oven temperature again to 220°C / 450°F and return the loaf to the oven, uncovered, for a further 10 - 15 minutes to allow it to form a crust.

Turn out carefully onto a wire rack and cover with a cloth to cool.

FOR THE WHOLE LOAF	
Energy Kcals	1606.00
Protein g	38.80
Fat g	45.14
Saturated fatty acids g	7.22
Monounsaturated fatty acids g	11.80
Polyunsaturated fatty acids g	20.44
Carbohydrate g	152.50
Total Sugars g	11.94
Sodium mg	2122.56
Fibre g	6.00

Festive Feasts -
Easter and Christmas

Rich Fruit Christmas Cake

Simnel Cake for Easter

Capon or Turkey Roast in Honey

Chicken or Turkey Stuffing

Rice Bread Sauce

Mince Pies

Pumpkin Pie for Thanksgiving

Christmas Pudding

This cake can be left exactly as it is or it can be iced with marzipan and white icing for Christmas or, since few families seem able to agree about icing on Christmas cakes, maybe you could just ice half of it and leave the other half untouched!

Rich Fruit Christmas Cake

An excellent cake which keeps well. It should feed 10 people amply over the Christmas holiday.

75 g	dried apricots, soaked for 30 minutes in boiling water if hard	3 oz
75 g	dried dates, soaked for 30 minutes in boiling water if hard	3 oz
75 g	dried prunes, soaked for 30 minutes in boiling water if hard	3 oz
10 mL	brandy	2 tbsp
	rind and juice of 2 lemons	
75 g	low-fat spread or butter	3 oz
2	medium eating apples, cored but not peeled, and minced in a food processor	2
2	medium pears, cored but not peeled, and minced in a food processor	2
125 g	rice flour	4½ oz
125 g	gram/chick pea flour	4½ oz
25 mL, hpd	gluten- and wheat-free baking powder	5 hpd tsp
5 mL	each ground ginger and ground cinnamon	1 tsp
50 g	ground almonds	2 oz
150 g	raisins	5 oz
150 g	currants	5 oz
150 g	golden raisins	5 oz
50 g	broken walnuts	2 oz
75 mL	coconut milk or ordinary milk	5 tbsp

Heat the oven to 150°C/300°F. Grease a 20 cm/8 inch tin and line it with greaseproof paper.

Chop the apricots, dates and prunes by hand or in a food processor. Mix them with the brandy, lemon juice and rind and set aside.

Cream the low-fat spread or butter with the minced apple and pear mixture, then beat in the dried fruits in their soaking liquid.

FOR THE WHOLE CAKE	
Energy Kcals	3758.15
Protein g	76.93
Fat g	104.59
Saturated fatty acids g	19.06
Monounsaturated fatty acids g	43.43
Polyunsaturated fatty acids g	45.99
Carbohydrate g	642.81
Total Sugars g	474.70
Sodium mg	2617.35
Fibre g	52.44

Sieve together the rice flour, gram flour, baking powder and spices. Fold them into the fruit mixture along with the ground almonds, raisins, currants, raisins and walnuts. Add the milk as required to make a stiff but moist dough.

Spoon into the cake tin and bake, uncovered, for 2 hours or until a skewer comes out of the middle clean.

Simnel Cake for Easter

The traditional way to make a simnel cake is to put the almond paste in a layer in the middle. However, since not everyone likes marzipan it may be better to bake it as an ordinary cake and merely ice it with the marzipan so it can be easily discarded. If you want to make the cake in the traditional way you will need to make the almond paste first.

225 g	icing or fine granulated sugar or icing and fine granulated sugar mixed (make sure the icing sugar is gluten free)	8 oz
225 g	ground almonds	8 oz
1	egg white	1
	juice of 1 lemon	
175 g	golden raisins	6 oz
50 g	mixed peel	2 oz
300 mL	dry cider	½ pint
225 g	sifted chick pea (gram) flour	8 oz
15 mL, hpd	baking powder	3 hpd tsp
100 g	dark brown sugar	4 oz
50 g	very soft butter	2 oz
50 g	raspberry jam	2 oz

Almond paste:

In an electric mixer, mix together the sugar and the almonds. Beat in the egg white and enough lemon juice to make a solid paste. Chill.

To make the cake:

Soak the raisins and the mixed peel in the cider for 1 hour.
Heat the oven to 180°C / 350°F.

FOR THE WHOLE CAKE	
Energy Kcals	4493.51
Protein g	106.77
Fat g	180.82
Saturated fatty acids g	40.20
Monounsaturated fatty acids g	91.28
Polyunsaturated fatty acids g	40.83
Carbohydrate g	643.68
Total Sugars g	528.93
Sodium mg	1638.35
Fibre g	46.69

Mix all the dry ingredients together in an electric mixer, then add the softened butter, fruit and peel and, gradually, the cider.

To make the cake traditionally, spoon half the cake mixture into a well-greased and lined 18-20 cm (7-8 inch) cake tin. Roll out 1/3 of the almond paste mixture into a round and lay it on top of the cake mixture. Spoon rest over the top. Alternatively, just spoon the cake mixture into the tin. Bake the cake for 40 - 45 minutes or until a skewer comes out clean. Take the cake out of the tin and cool it on a rack.

When the cake is quite cold, spread it thinly with the raspberry jam. Roll out the rest of the almond paste (use plenty of icing sugar and wrap the paste around the roller). Cover the cake, pressing the extra down the side to cover the sides. Use any offcuts to make little balls with which to decorate the cake.

Capon or Turkey Roast in Honey

Serves 10

A very dramatic old English recipe - great for Christmas or any other festive occasion.

2.5 kg	capon or small turkey	5 lb
50 g	the liver from the bird, chopped	2 oz
75 g	butter	3 oz
1	medium onion, finely chopped	1
	large handful of parsley, finely chopped	
75 g	cooking apple, peeled and chopped small	3 oz
75 g	plump raisins	3 oz
	rind and juice of 1 1/2 lemons	
75 g	ground almonds	3 oz
75 g	cooked white rice	3 oz
5 mL	ground ginger	1 tsp
5 mL	salt	1 tsp
2.5 mL	black pepper	1/2 tsp
1	egg	1
30 mL	honey	2 tbsp

Remove the giblets from the bird, retain the liver and discard (or make stock from) the rest.

Melt 25 g (1 oz) of the butter in a saucepan, add the onion, chopped liver and parsley and fry gently until the onion is soft and the liver firm. Take off the heat and add the apple, raisins, lemon, almonds, cooked rice, seasoning and egg. Mix well.

Stuff the bird at both ends and secure with a skewer. Place in a roasting pan. Melt the honey with the rest of the butter and spoon the mixture over the bird; as it cools it will cling fairly well to the skin. Leave the bird to marinate in the honey in the refrigerator for 24 hours, spooning over any excess mixture every now and then.

To cook, heat the oven to 180°C / 350°F. Roast the bird, uncovered, basting it frequently with the honey and butter mixture, for approximately 20 minutes per 500 g (1 lb) - 1 hour and 40 minutes. The skin will gradually turn black and shiny in contrast to the very white meat underneath. Serve either warm or cold.

PER SERVING	
Energy Kcals	513.52
Protein g	35.32
Fat g	34.00
Saturated fatty acids g	11.21
Monounsaturated fatty acids g	15.18
Polyunsaturated fatty acids g	5.76
Carbohydrate g	17.29
Total Sugars g	10.82
Sodium mg	266.60
Fibre g	1.06

Chicken or Turkey Stuffing

Enough to stuff a bird large enough to feed 10 people

Millet is another cereal grain which is high in fibre but gluten free. It is a small, hardish round grain which needs long cooking (excellent in a stuffing) and also used as a flour in some commercial wheat- and gluten-free flour mixes.

200 g	whole millet grain	7 oz
500 mL	water	18 fl oz
30 mL	olive oil	2 tbsp
300 g	onions, peeled and chopped finely	10½ oz
2	sticks celery, chopped small	2
25 g	sun-dried tomatoes, chopped very small	1 oz
6	bacon slices, chopped small	6
150 g	raw chicken liver, chopped	5½ oz
50 g	whole cashew nuts	2 oz
2	eggs	2
200 mL	medium sherry	7 fl oz
	sea salt	
	freshly ground black pepper	

Put the millet grain in a large saucepan with the water, bring to the boil and simmer gently for 10 minutes. Turn off the heat, cover the pan and leave it to steam for a further 10 minutes. (N.B. These instructions are for natural, untouched millet grain. Check on your pack as if it has already been processed it may need less cooking or less water.)

Meanwhile heat the oil in a pan and add the onion, celery, sun-dried tomatoes and bacon. Cook briskly, without burning, for 5 - 10 minutes or until the vegetables are soft. Add the chicken livers and continue to cook for a further 3 - 4 minutes.

Take off the heat and add the nuts, eggs and sherry, then the millet. Mix very thoroughly, then season to taste.

The stuffing is now ready to go into the bird. If you have too much, make little balls out of what is over and roast them for 15 - 20 minutes on the oven tray beside the bird.

PER SERVING	
Energy Kcals	294.66
Protein g	9.83
Fat g	17.29
Saturated fatty acids g	5.33
Polyunsaturated fatty acids g	2.60
Monounsaturated fatty acids g	8.67
Carbohydrate g	19.53
Total Sugars g	2.94
Sodium mg	398.52
Fibre g	0.75

Rice Bread Sauce

Serves 8

100 g	white pudding rice	4 oz
900 mL	milk	1½ pints
1 - 2	medium onions stuck with around 12 whole cloves	1 - 2
	salt and 10 black peppercorns	

Put the rice in a pan with the milk and the onion or onions stuck with the cloves and the peppercorns. Bring slowly to the boil and simmer very gently, taking care it does not stick or burn, for 20 - 30 minutes or until the rice is quite soft. Remove the cloves from the onions and purée the milky rice in a food processor. Depending on how strong an onion flavour you like, purée the onions with the mixture or remove them first. Season to taste with salt and reheat gently in a pan or (better) in a microwave before serving.

PER SERVING	
Energy Kcals	123.63
Protein g	4.68
Fat g	4.48
Saturated fatty acids g	2.83
Monounsaturated fatty acids g	1.36
Polyunsaturated fatty acids g	0.13
Carbohydrate g	16.36
Total Sugars g	6.23
Sodium mg	62.25
Fibre g	0.18

Mince Pies

This mixture will make 1 large pie to feed 10 - 12 or about 12 individual pies

This mincemeat has no added sugar so although it is rich it is not as cloying as many mince pie mixtures.

375 g	sifted chick pea (gram) flour	13 oz
25 g	pale brown sugar	1 oz
150 g	dairy free margarine	5 oz
100 g	raisins	4 oz
100 g	golden raisins	4 oz
100 g	currants	4 oz
50 g	glacé cherries	2 oz
50 g	mixed peel	2 oz
5 mL	ground ginger	1 tsp
5 mL	ground nutmeg	1 tsp
2.5 mL	ground mace	½ tsp
10 mL	ground cinnamon	2 tsp
50 g	vegetable suet	2 oz
1	medium-sized, sharp eating apple	1
1	orange	1
150 mL	brandy or whisky	5 fl oz

Mix the sugar into the flour, then cut and rub in the fat until it is well crumbed. Add about 180 mL / 12 tablespoons of cold water and mix to a dough. It needs to be pretty sticky if it is not to crumble. Use extra gram flour to dust a board, then roll out as normal.

Line a 24 cm/9 inch pie plate with the pastry (if it tears just patch it with extra paste), line with foil, weight with beans and bake blind for 10 minutes in a moderate oven (180°C/350°F). Remove the beans and foil and continue to bake for a further 5 minutes, then cool.

Alternatively, line mince pie tins with the pastry (you will probably get 12 - 15 out of the mixture) in which case you do not need to bake them blind.

Mix all the dried fruits with the spices and suet. Put the apple, cored and quartered but not peeled, and the orange, cut into quarters but not peeled, in a food processor and purée. Add this

PER SERVING	
Energy Kcals	123.63
Protein g	4.68
Fat g	4.48
Saturated fatty acids g	2.83
Monounsaturated fatty acids g	1.36
Polyunsaturated fatty acids g	0.13
Carbohydrate g	16.36
Total Sugars g	6.23
Sodium mg	62.25
Fibre g	0.18

PER PORTION	
Energy Kcals	432.93
Protein g	8.68
Fat g	19.03
Saturated fatty acids g	8.27
Polyunsaturated fatty acids g	3.44
Monounsaturated fatty acids g	7.08
Carbohydrate g	52.55
Total Sugars g	34.34
Sodium mg	162.40
Fibre g	5.42

mixture to the dried fruit along with the brandy or whisky. Mix well, cover and set aside for 2 - 24 hours.

When ready to make the pies, mix the fruit mixture well together then fill the pastry shells with it. Top the pies with a lid or with a lattice work of pastry and decorate as you feel inclined. You may also brush the top with egg.

Otherwise just bake in a moderately hot oven (180°C/375°F) for approximately 15 minutes or until the crust is lightly browned and crisp.

You can sprinkle the pies with sugar when they come out of the oven.

Pumpkin Pie for Thanksgiving

Serves 8

Many people use ready-made pumpkin pie mix but I have found that the extra effort in using fresh pumpkin is well worth while.

200 g	sifted chick pea (gram) flour	7 oz
100 g	butter	4 oz
60 mL	water	4 tbsp
350 g	mashed pumpkin flesh - it is best to steam the pumpkin pieces and then mash the flesh like a potato	12 oz
125 g	demerara sugar or dark brown sugar	5 oz
15 mL	molasses	1 tbsp
2.5 mL	ground nutmeg	½ tsp
2.5 mL	ground cinnamon	½ tsp
2.5 mL	salt	½ tsp
2	eggs	2
120 mL	whipping cream	4 fl oz
50 g	broken pecan nuts	2 oz

Ginger meringue topping - optional:

2	egg whites	2
50 g	icing sugar, gluten free	2 oz
5 mL	lemon juice	1 tsp
50 g	stem ginger, chopped	2 oz

Heat the oven to 180°C / 350°F.

   Rub the butter into the flour then mix to a soft dough with the water. Roll out the paste and line a 20 cm / 8 inch pie plate. Line it with foil and weight it with beans or rice then bake it blind - 10 minutes with the foil and beans, then another 10 minutes without.

   Lower the oven to 160°C / 325°F.

   In a bowl mix the pumpkin flesh with the sugar, molasses and spices. Whisk the eggs with the cream and add them to the pumpkin mixture, then stir in the nuts. Spoon the mixture into the pre-baked pie shell and cook for 45 - 50 minutes or until the custard is set.

Optional ginger meringue:

Whisk the egg whites with the icing sugar and lemon juice until very stiff and shiny. Fold in the chopped ginger and spread the meringue mixture over the cooked pie. Return to a slightly hotter oven for 15 - 20 minutes just to set and colour the meringue. Serve warm or cold.

INCLUDING THE MERINGUE TOPPING	
Energy Kcals	405.53
Protein g	9.17
Fat g	25.05
Saturated fatty acids g	12.40
Monounsaturated fatty acids g	8.76
Polyunsaturated fatty acids g	3.12
Carbohydrate g	39.12
Total Sugars g	26.69
Sodium mg	202.29
Fibre g	3.41

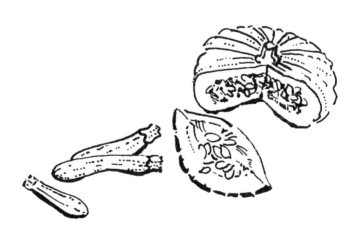

Christmas Pudding

Serves 10

If any of the fruits seem rather hard soak them for 10 - 15 minutes in boiling water before making the pudding. You can cook - or at least reheat - the pudding in the microwave, but it will not be as light.

50 g	raisins	2 oz
50 g	golden raisins	2 oz
50 g	currants	2 oz
25 g	mixed peel	1 oz
25 g	ready-to-eat prunes	1 oz
25 g	dried apricots	1 oz
25 g	dried dates	1 oz
100 g	sharp eating apples, peeled, cored and chopped	4 oz
2.5 mL	ground ginger	½ tsp
2.5 mL	ground cinnamon plus 1 mL / ¼ tsp ground mace	½ tsp
25 g	vegetable or meat suet	1 oz
25 g	flaked almonds	1 oz
50 g	chick pea (gram) flour	2 oz
50 g	rice flour	2 oz
2	eggs	2
60 mL	brandy or orange juice, or a combination of the two	4 tbsp
45 mL	milk	3 tbsp

PER SERVING	
Energy Kcals	174.05
Protein g	4.29
Fat g	5.56
Saturated fatty acids g	1.89
Monounsaturated fatty acids g	2.30
Polyunsaturated fatty acids g	1.00
Carbohydrate g	23.98
Total Sugars g	17.27
Sodium mg	36.38
Fibre g	1.87

Mix the fruits with the spices, the suet and the nuts. Sieve the gram flour and add it to the fruit mixture with the rice flour. Beat the eggs with the brandy and the milk and stir it into the mixture. Spoon the mixture into a pudding basin, cover with doubled greaseproof paper and tie with a string or rubber bands. Put the basin in a deep pan, pour in water to half way up the bowl, cover the pan tightly and simmer for 4 - 5 hours, checking periodically to make sure that the water has not dried up.

Resources Directory

Canadian Celiac Chapter Addresses

ALBERTA

Calgary Chapter
7-11th Street NE
Calgary, AB T2E 4Z2
Ph: (403) 237-0304
Fx: (403) 269-9626

Edmonton Chapter
Room 5R17
11111 Jasper Avenue
Edmonton, AB T5K 0L4
Ph/Fx: (780) 482-8967

BRITISH COLUMBIA

Kamloops Chapter
116 River Road
Kamloops, BC V2C 4P9
Ph: (250) 374-6185

Kelowna Chapter
2468 Thacker Road
Kelowna, BC V2C 4P9

Vancouver Chapter
1212 West Broadway,
Suite 306
Vancouver, BC V6H 3V1
Ph: (604) 948-2750

Victoria Chapter
P.O. Box 5765, Station B
Victoria, BC V8R 6S8

MANITOBA

Manitoba Chapter
825 Sherbrook St.
Winnipeg, MB R3A 1M5
Ph: (204) 772-6979

NEW BRUNSWICK

Fredericton Chapter
527 Beaverbrook Court, Suite 226
Fredericton, NB E3B 1X6
Ph: (506) 450-4357

Moncton Chapter
P.O. Box 1576
Moncton, NB E1C 9X4

Saint John Chapter
454 Elmore Crescent
Saint John, NB E2M 3C1
Ph: (506) 672-4454

NEWFOUNDLAND

St. John's Chapter
262 Freshwater Road
St. John's, NFLD A1B 1B8

NOVA SCOTIA

Halifax Chapter
P.O. Box 9104, Station A
Halifax, NS B3K 5M7
Ph: (902) 464-9222

ONTARIO

Hamilton Chapter
P.O. Box 65580
Dundas Postal Outlet
Dundas, ON L9H 6Y6
Ph: (905) 572-6775

Kitchener/Waterloo Chapter
153 Frederick Street, Suite 118
Kitchener, ON N2H 2M3

London Chapter
P.O. Box 198
Dorchester, ON N0L 1G0

Ottawa Chapter
Box 39035, Billings P.O.
Ottawa, ON K1H 1A1
Ph: (613) 786-1335

Quinte Chapter
P.O. Box 20104
Belleville, ON K8N 5V1

St. Catharines Chapter
Grantham P.O. Box 20193
St. Catharines, ON L2M 7W7

Sudbury Chapter
P.O. Box 2794, Station A
Sudbury, ON P3A 5J3

Thunder Bay & District Chapters
P.O. Box 20100
Green Acres Plaza P/O
Thunder Bay, ON P7E 6P2
Ph: (807) 346-8190

PRINCE EDWARD ISLAND

Charlottetown Chapter
290 Lidstone Street
Summerside, PEI C1N 3G5

QUEBEC

Montreal Chapter
614-21 Lakeshore Drive
Montreal, QC H9S 5N2

SASKATCHEWAN

Regina Chapter
P.O. Box 1773
Regina, SK S4P 3C6

Saskatoon Chapter
P.O. Box 8953
Saskatoon, SK S7K 6S7

GLUTEN FREE DISTRIBUTORS

DE-RO-MA
1118 Berlier
Laval, QC H7L 3R9
Ph: (450) 990-5694
Fx: (450) 629-4781
Toll Free: 1-800-363-3438
e-mail: deroma@odyssee.net
www.cosmo2000.ca/deroma

El Peto Products
2-41 Shoemaker Street
Kitchener, ON N2E 3G9
Ph: (519) 748-5211
Fx: (519) 748-5279
Toll Free: 1-800-387-4064
e-mail: elpeto@golden.net

ENER-G Foods
5960 First Avenue South
P.O. Box 84487
Seattle, Washington USA
98124-5787
Ph: (206) 767-6660
Fx: (206) 764-3398
Toll Free: 1-800-331-5222

Kingsmill Foods Company Ltd.
17-1399 Kennedy Road
Scarborough, ON M1P 2L6
Ph: (416) 755-1124
Fx: (416) 755-4486

Kinnickinnick Foods
10306-112 Street
Edmonton, AB T5K 1N1
Ph: (780) 424-2900
Fx: (780) 421-0456
Toll Free: 1-877-503-4466
e-mail: info@kinnikinnick.com
www.kinnikinnick.com

Liv-N-Well Distributors
1-7900 River Road
Richmond, BC V6X 1X7
Ph: (604) 270-8474
Fx: (604) 270-1147
e-mail: www.liv-n-well.com

Nelson David of Canada
Celimix Products
101-193 Dumoulin Street
Winnipeg, MB R2H 0E4
Ph: (204) 237-9161
Fx: (204) 989-0384

Rice Innovations Inc.
8175 Winston Churchill Blvd.
Norval, ON L0P 1K0
Ph: (905) 451-7423
Fx: (905) 453-8137

Specialty Food Shop
555 University Avenue
Toronto, ON M5G 1X8
Ph: (416) 977-4360
Fx: (416) 977-8394
Toll Free: 1-800-737-7976
e-mail: sfs@sickkids.on.ca

Specialty Food Shop
875 Main Street West
Hamilton, ON L8S 4P9
Ph: (905) 528-4707
Fx: (905) 528-5625
Toll Free: 1-800-737-7976

INDEX